T0360733

Employment Relations and Ethnic Minority Enterprise

This book is the first piece of extensive research studying employment relations in ethnic Chinese small businesses in Britain. It contributes to existing knowledge in three respects. Empirically, it examines the nature of employment relations in the ethnic Chinese restaurant sector in the UK context, a hitherto under-explored area. The study adds new knowledge to the study of employment relations in ethnic minority small firms. Theoretically, it draws out the concept of 'ethnic twist', which denotes how the conflict between different group members from the same ethnicity shapes patterns of shop floor behaviours, revealing the heterogeneity of people from the same ethnic origins. Methodologically, the research demonstrates the continued importance of the ethnographic approach in studying workplace relations.

Additionally, we see lots of literature discussing overseas Chinese businesses in terms of cultural resources, business development, level of integration and structural constraints. Surprisingly little is published on interpretations of small firm workplace relations. This book might illuminate future studies to explore management practices and employment relationships in ethnic Chinese small businesses in different national environments and industry sectors. It will be of interest to researchers, academics and students in the fields of employment relations, human resource management and organisational behaviour.

Xisi Li is a Senior Researcher in the Business School at the Peking University Founder Group Co., Ltd.

Routledge Focus on Business and Management

The fields of business and management have grown exponentially as areas of research and education. This growth presents challenges for readers trying to keep up with the latest important insights. Routledge Focus on Business and Management presents small books on big topics and how they intersect with the world of business research.

Individually, each title in the series provides coverage of a key academic topic, whilst collectively, the series forms a comprehensive collection across the business disciplines.

Liminality in Organization Studies
Theory and Method
Maria Rita Tagliaventi

Ephemeral Retailing
Pop-up Stores in a Postmodern Consumption Era
Ghalia Boustani

Effective Workforce Development
A Concise Guide for HR and Line Managers
Antonios Panagiotakopoulos

Women, Work and Migration
Nursing in Australia
Diane van den Broek and Dimitria Groutsis

Employment Relations and Ethnic Minority Enterprise
An Ethnography of Chinese Restaurants in the UK
Xisi Li

For more information about this series, please visit: www.routledge.com/ Routledge-Focus-on-Business-and-Management/book-series/FBM

Employment Relations and Ethnic Minority Enterprise

An Ethnography of Chinese Restaurants in the UK

Xisi Li

Routledge
Taylor & Francis Group

NEW YORK AND LONDON

First published 2020
by Routledge
52 Vanderbilt Avenue, New York, NY 10017

and by Routledge
2 Park Square, Milton Park, Abingdon, Oxon, OX14 4RN

Routledge is an imprint of the Taylor & Francis Group, an informa business

© 2020 Taylor & Francis

Library of Congress Cataloging-in-Publication Data
A catalog record for this book has been requested

ISBN: 978-0-367-32113-0 (hbk)
ISBN: 978-0-429-31666-1 (ebk)

Typeset in Times New Roman
by Apex CoVantage, LLC

Contents

Acknowledgements

I want to thank Dr Robert Wapshott and Professor Jason Heyes. They were my supervisors during my PhD study at the University of Sheffield. I have been extremely grateful for their selfless and generous assistance.

I thank my family for their economic and moral support.

Preface

Studies of employment relations in ethnic minority small firms have long focused on the South Asian and black communities. While the richness of these accounts has contributed much to our understanding of employment relations in small firms both relating to members of minority communities and more widely, there remains scope for engaging with a greater diversity of minority ethnic communities in the UK context. Specifically, there has not been any extensive research focusing on the ethnic Chinese population. The study aims to examine the nature of employment relations in the ethnic Chinese restaurant sector to address the current research gap.

The study is located within a rich ethnographic tradition. The fieldwork for the current study consisted of participant observation of restaurant work for a period of seven months spent in two ethnic Chinese restaurants in Sheffield. The researcher worked as a full-time front area waiter and a full-time kitchen assistant. The fieldwork enabled the researcher to develop a nuanced understanding of workplace behaviours. By focusing on four different aspects—the product market, the labour market, multi-cultural workforces and the interaction between informality and ethnicity, this research thoroughly explains how management practices and employment relationships are influenced in the UK's ethnic Chinese restaurant sector.

This research contributes to existing knowledge in three respects. Empirically, it examines the nature of employment relations in the ethnic Chinese restaurant sector in the UK context, a hitherto under-explored area. The study adds new knowledge to the study of employment relations in ethnic minority small firms. Theoretically, it draws out the concept of 'ethnic twist', which denotes how the conflict between different group members from the same ethnicity shapes patterns of shop floor behaviours, revealing the heterogeneity of people from the same ethnic origin. Methodologically, the research demonstrates the continued importance of the ethnographic approach in studying workplace relations.

1 Setting the Background

Small and medium-sized enterprises (SMEs) are independent businesses with limited size, managed by its owner or co-owners and having a small market share. BIS (2014) defines small firms as those with a maximum of 49 employees and medium-sized firms as those with between 50 and 249 employees. According to BIS (2018), small and medium-sized businesses accounted for 99.9% of all enterprises in the UK. SMEs provided 16.3 million jobs, making up 60% of all private sector employment. China's SMEs comprised nearly 98% of all firms, accounting for 80% of employment and 58% of total GDP (Ecovis, 2017). In America, firms with fewer than 50 employees made up over 99% of all businesses (ASE, 2016). Given the essential role of small firms in modern economies, the study of management practices and employment relationships in small firms is a crucial component in understanding work and organisations.

Shaping Employment Relations in Small Firms

The focus of small firms with distinct importance from larger companies emerged at the beginning of the 1970s. Early studies presented two polarised perspectives around how employment relationships and working lives are experienced in small firms, which is the 'small is beautiful' versus 'bleak house' (Wilkinson, 1999). The 'small is beautiful' scenario was represented by the Bolton Committee Report (1971). This view suggested that small firms could facilitate close and harmonious working relationships. The physical environment in small firms might be worse than in big companies, but most people still preferred to work in a small firm as there were fewer problems in communication and management practices would be adjusted to match individuals. Additionally, small firms provided more intrinsic rewards. Although their average wage was lower than in large organisations, harmonious social relationships and low levels of conflict led people to gain an alternative type of satisfaction and motivation (Ingham, 1970).

The second is the bleak house scenario represented by Sisson (1993). This perspective suggested that workers in small businesses generally received fewer financial rewards than in big firms. Due to lack of resources, small businesses could rarely employ rigorous and integrated management practices. Without pressure from the trade union, workers were often treated in unfair ways. Scott and Rainnie (1982) argued that the context of small firms was not a 'better environment' for workers as depicted by the Bolton Report.

These two contrasting perspectives laid the foundation in exploring working lives and employment relationships in small firms. However, they both widely shared the understanding that size itself determined how behaviours in small firms were different from large companies. With further research into studying employment relations in small firms, it suggested that relations between owner-managers and workers are complex and contested, rather than size-determined (Wilkinson, 1999; Marlow, 2002; Tsai et al., 2007; Atkinson, 2008). A variety of factors, both external and internal, contribute to shaping employment relationships and management practices in small firms.

Rainnie (1989) classified small firms into four types according to the extent of their dependence on large firms. The dominant market position of large companies could exert significant influence on labour management practices in small businesses, directly or indirectly. Owner-managers' choices in these small businesses were considerably constrained. They were forced to conduct tight control and brutal management over labour in response to the market pressure, which limited the scope for employees to contest management. Such product market environment determined how labour was managed in small firms. Goss (1991a) emphasised the essential role of the labour market in the management process in small firms. He identified four types of control strategies based on the dependence of employers and employees. Workers' abilities to resist management and the dynamics of workplace relations were contingent upon their labour market positions.

The models advanced the understanding of employment relations in small firms by considering the influences of both size and external variables. However, they have been criticised as being extremely deterministic by stating that structural factors dominated the management practices (Ram, 1994; Holliday, 1995; Moule, 1998). The internal forces played a central role in shaping shop floor dynamics and workplace relations. Ram's (1994) research illustrated how orders were negotiated between owners and workers during the day-to-day life on the shop floor. He demonstrated that employment relations in small firms were largely shaped by the nature of informal, ongoing everyday negotiations. The struggle between owners and workers during the bargaining process was inherent in small firms, and negotiation between the two parties was continuous and contingent upon diverse situations. Moule (1998) further suggested that in situations where small firms were dominated by larger companies and competitive pressures, there remained scope for owner-managers and workers to engage in informal bargaining. The impact of external structures was mediated through the shop floor dynamics on a bargaining basis.

Ram et al. (2001) defined the informality as the working process based mainly on unwritten customs and the tacit understandings arising from the interaction between employers and employees at work. It is possible to identify that informality distinguishes employment relations in small firms from those in larger organisations (Marlow, 2003; Gilman and Edwards, 2008). Human resource management practices in small firms show procedural informality on ad hoc bases in organising and completing tasks (Barrett, 1999; Wapshott and Mallett, 2013). Orders are subject to a constant informal negotiation between owner-managers and workers, which revealed the nature of the internal political process of management (Scase, 2005; Dundon and Wilkinson, 2009). As the order is negotiated in an informal environment, these ongoing, everyday interactions produce forms of mutual adjustment between owner-managers and workers (Nadin and Cassell, 2007; Ram, 1999). The bargained nature shapes the dynamics of accommodation with influences under varying degrees of both internal and external pressures (Wapshott and Mallett, 2016).

Apart from the market constraints, studies also have examined how laws and regulations influence small firms' behaviours (Heyes and Gray, 2004; Kitching, 2006; Carter et al., 2009). These studies examined how and why small firm owners adapted to regulatory change and the subsequent consequences on labour management practices and employment relations. Edwards et al. (2004) indicated that two main structural reasons explained why small firms might experience considerable effects following the introduction of types of regulations. First, small businesses are likely to pay workers lower wages than larger firms. As a result, it is expected that particular laws, such as the NMW, would affect small businesses more significantly. Second, because small firms usually have little to deploy in terms of capital and human resources, they would be more vulnerable in the face of the pressures caused by regulatory laws compared to larger companies. Additionally, the decision to operate formally to comply with the laws was strictly dependent upon firms' profitability, which itself was not common in the small firm economy (Ram et al., 2007). Management in small firms are affected by laws and regulations to various extents according to their market positions, internal structures, resources, etc. (Gilman et al., 2002; Edwards et al., 2006; Carter et al., 2009). Regulatory impacts interact with the specific business context to shape patterns of responses. It is necessary to integrate the regulations, the environment and the dynamics of informality to examine management practices and employment relationships in small firms (Arrowsmith et al., 2003).

Employment relations in small firms are, therefore, complex and heterogeneous (Marlow, 2005). Understanding employment relations in small firms requires sensitivity to external constraints while acknowledging how internal forces shape the process. Although external factors might have a strong influence on labour management practices, they interact with informality and negotiated order in shaping shop floor dynamics and employment relationships in small firms. The tensions between factors are negotiated on their everyday practices, which leaves space for strategic choice (Child, 1997).

Having realised the influence of both external and internal factors, an integrated approach to analyse employment relations in small firms has been developed (Harney and Dundon, 2006; Gilman and Edwards, 2008). The core argument of the integrated approach is to focus on the interplay between the internal dynamics within a firm and their external constraints. The frameworks synthesise key dimensions that influence labour management in small firms. These analytical frameworks serve to guide empirical research in understanding how the context of the different firms can shape patterns of employment relations, which reflects the context-sensitive view in interpreting shop floor behaviours and employment relationships in small firms (Ram and Edwards, 2010).

Employment Relations in Ethnic Minority Small Firms

The study of ethnic minority businesses has been playing a significant role in advancing knowledge in the field of employment relations in small firms. For instance, research conducted by Ram (1994) and Holliday (1995) revealed the bargained nature on the shop floor. Among all the ethnic minority groups, the South Asian community (mainly Indian, Pakistani and Bangladesh) has been mainly studied. There was a tradition for South Asians working in the restaurant sector (Ram et al., 2000; Barrett et al., 2002). The reason why so many South Asians engaged in the restaurant sector was believed to be the result of a historical disadvantage and the discrimination that ethnic minorities had been facing (Ohri and Faruqi, 1988; Ram, 1994). Due to the kinds of racism and discrimination, ethnic entrepreneurs often found their choices constrained by the white-dominated society (Ram, 1992). The historical reason pushed them into particular sectors because of the absence of alternatives; the restaurant sector was one of them (Ram et al., 2002). The racial context functioned and influenced the traditions of ethnic minority small firms to significant degrees.

Employment in these ethnic minority restaurants was largely organised by kinship and family ties. Kinship and family ties were regarded as the primary resource for the development of South Asian ethnic enterprises (Ward, 1987; Jones et al., 2006; Carter, 2011). This was seen as an essential factor for ethnic minority firms to survive due to lack of resources (Ram and Holliday, 1993). Family members worked as providers of capital and labour, which was crucial to prepare and operate a restaurant (Ram et al., 2000). Familial networks could effectively facilitate firms to cope with the competitive and unpredictable pressures from the product market and the uncertainties deriving from labour supply (Ram et al., 2007). Family members and kinship ties were a means of overcoming racial obstacles in the market externally and a source of cheap and flexible labour in supporting business development internally.

Apart from the support from family members, another key feature within the ethnic minority restaurant sector is the ethnicity network and community support. Co-ethnic workers were widely recruited within South Asian restaurants (Ram et al., 2000). Werbner (1994) demonstrated that the establishment of networks in Pakistani enterprises was always largely dependent on the community itself. Members of their communities shared common needs and cultures, which helped to consolidate employer-employee relationships to ease the management (Ram and Hillin, 1994). One of the dramatic advantages arising from their social networks and community support was 'trust'. Co-ethnic employees were often deemed to be more 'trustworthy' than other employees, and this facilitated the labour control process (Werbner, 1984; Ward, 1991).

There is no doubt that the ethno-cultural factors had considerable influences on labour management practices in ethnic minority small firms. However, it is also argued that ethnic businesses are shaped by the wider political-economic environment (Barrett et al., 2002). The study of employment relations and entrepreneurship in ethnic minority small firms should take a 'mixed embeddedness' view (Kloosterman et al., 1999; Kloosterman, 2010). The key point of the concept is that ethnic businesses must be examined under the wider political-economic environment as well as in the social-cultural capital of their own communities. Research should not isolate ethnic enterprises from the surrounding environment. Activities in ethnic minority small firms arise from the interaction between economic and political processes rather than a distinct cultural issue for developing their businesses and managing labour (Ram et al., 2017a). Analysis of employment relations in ethnic businesses has to be integrated with socio-economic-political factors to explain their practices.

By locating ethnic minority firms in a wider context, the effect of informality significantly interacted with ethnicity in shaping shop floor behaviours. As ethnic small firms generally operated in marginal sectors with strong market competition and low profitability, family and kinship ties reduced their economic pressure and sectorial constraints to a large extent, and the employment of family members facilitated informal practices in management (Ram et al., 2002). Because ethnic workers normally had either no or very low-level formal qualifications, they faced a substantial barrier in the labour market. The ethnic ties provided them with the opportunity to get employed and meanwhile gave owner-managers advantages to tighten the control and deploy the low-paid ethnic workers as resources (Ram, 1994; Edwards et al., 2016). In the face of laws and regulations, some of the ethnic minority small firms in order to survive paid workers significantly less than the NMW (Jones et al., 2006). Some businesses have responded to the NMW by employing undocumented workers from ethnic backgrounds (Ram et al., 2017b). Informality took different forms within the ethnic background in responding to the introduction of NMW and other external pressures. Thus, it is necessary to integrate informality with ethnicity to understand how these two variables interact with each other in shaping workplace behaviours and management practices in ethnic minority businesses.

The number of businesses owned by other ethnic minority communities in the UK has grown substantially during the past few decades (Ram and Jones, 2008). However, academic research has yet to extensively explore these new groups, and people had a limited understanding of their business development and employment structures (Jones et al., 2010). The conventional understanding of Britain's migrant and ethnic minority population represented by the South Asian community should give way to an increased number of diverse groups (Vertovec, 2007).

In responding to the call, Jones et al. (2010) examined the dynamics of Somali business formation and development in Leicester; Sepulveda et al. (2011) focused on the economic activities of six communities in London to explore their economic positions and social activities. It is suggested that ethnic minority businesses not only contributed to economic growth, but also facilitated social processes by providing employment for local people and supporting community needs (Hall et al., 2017; Jones et al., 2019). These studies improved both empirical and conceptual understandings of diverse new migrant enterprise activities in Britain. Future studies to explore ethnic minority businesses, therefore, should focus on a wider range of ethnic communities and compare the experiences of different ethnic minority groups (Jones et al., 2006).

The Ethnic Chinese Community in the UK Context

The Chinese Diaspora in the UK

The Chinese in Britain have diverse origins and cultural backgrounds. Seamen were the first group of Chinese to the UK during the 1850s. They were recruited to develop maritime trade in Asia. A large number of Chinese people from Hong Kong started to arrive in Britain after the Second World War. The immigration wave was believed to be due to economic deterioration in Hong Kong's rural areas (Chiu, 1991). More Hong Kong immigrants arrived in Britain between the late 1950s and the late 1960s. They came to Britain mainly to earn a living. Against this background, Hong Kong people became the largest Chinese group in Britain (Chan and Chan, 1997). According to the 1991 Census (OPCS, 1992), the total number of people in Britain with Chinese origin in 1991 was 156,900. Those who were born in Hong Kong were the largest group and accounted for one-third of the population. British-born Chinese accounted for 28%. The percentage of people from mainland China was only 12%.

The UK Chinese community has increased significantly in recent years and become more diverse. By 2011, the Chinese population grew to 400,000 in England and Wales, accounting for 0.7% of the entire population (ONS, 2015). This was primarily explained by the labour immigration from China's Fujian and Guangdong provinces. Furthermore, there had been increased number of Chinese students. The Chinese student population generally kept stable from 1995 to 2000, around 5,000 per year. However, the student number began to increase significantly from 2001: from 20,000 in 2001 to 50,000 in 2004. In 2016, it jumped to 95,090 (UKCISA, 2019). According to the statistics, 79% of the ethnic Chinese population rise between 2001 and 2011 was due to immigration from Mainland China (Mok and Platt, 2018). As most of the migration was from Mainland China, the Chinese community traditionally dominated by Hong Kong people has shifted to a society in which Mainland Chinese has become the majority.

Early first generation ethnic Chinese in the UK mainly operated their businesses in the food and catering industry, which was the survival strategy for the historical discrimination they had encountered (Mok and Platt, 2018). Since then, they have been in the tradition of working in the restaurant sector with less ethnic embeddedness and integration to the mainstream economy. Ninety percent of Chinese workers took part in the catering industry by self-employment (House of Commons, 1985). Based on a recent survey, it was found that over three-quarters of male Chinese worked in the restaurant sector (Clark and Drinkwater, 2010). In large cities, they located together to form a group-based 'China Town' to mainly attract Chinese customers. For those who run their restaurants in small cities, it was believed to be the strategy to avoid co-ethnic competition (Luk, 2009). Chan et al. (2007) suggested that by organising their businesses in the catering industry, ethnic Chinese could generate long-term stable profits. The supply and demand relations for Chinese working in the catering industry secured the advantage of their market position, which kept them at a distance from the mainstream market.

Characteristics of the Ethnic Chinese Community in the UK Context

Compared to other ethnic minority groups within the UK context, the Chinese community was believed to be unique because it was generally regarded as a relatively 'invisible' community (House of Commons, 1985). The concept denotes that Chinese occasionally participated in social and political connection to the main society. Furthermore, the Chinese were identified as rarely utilising social services (Rochelle and Marks, 2011). As a result, Chinese people have always been perceived as having sufficient resources to meet their needs (Rochelle and Shardlow, 2013). This is explained mainly by two reasons.

The first is their cultural background. The Chinese community in the UK was rarely concerned with developing social relationships and interacting with people outside its community (Watson, 1977; Chau and Yu, 2001). Runnymede Trust (1986) noted that the Chinese community was a silent and self-sufficient community; they preferred self-reliance within the family and community. This was largely attributed to the cultural tradition of the Chinese with its emphasis on self-help and mutual aid, which led them to a reluctance to gain support outside the Chinese community. Due to following their traditional values, the Chinese group tended to exclude themselves from mainstream society. Thus, this cultural characterisation to a certain extent suggested that the Chinese group was responsible for their 'social exclusion'.

The second reason relates to their economic activities. As stated above, ethnic Chinese in the UK have the tradition of running their businesses in the catering industry. Although there had been a significant increase for Chinese immigrants holding higher qualifications in recent years, this did not change their economic structure of working in the restaurant sector substantially (Clark and Drinkwater, 2010). The continuous rise of Chinese students over the past decade maintained a high level of customer demand. Ethnic penalty (Heath et al., 2008) and lack of ethnic embeddedness (Clark and Drinkwater, 2002) were, therefore, not serious problems in the Chinese community. A fully satisfying market position in the catering sector gave them no need to move to a mainstream market and compete with whites (Tong et al., 2011).

Although activities of the ethnic Chinese group were largely conducted at the community level, the solidarity and cohesion between group members were much weaker than people might assume. Many Chinese within the UK context indeed experienced 'double social exclusion': they were not fully integrated into the social mainstream and maintained a distance from each other inside the community (Chau and Yu, 2001). This was primarily caused by the strategies they chose to operate their businesses. Due to the competitive relationship, Chinese restaurant owners tended to hide information from one another and attempted to avoid visiting their potential rivals' workplaces and interacting with them (Taylor, 1987). They always held the idea to prevent potential rivals from gathering information about their market situations. Information was rarely disclosed because this might threaten their market positions (Chau and Yu, 2001). A trust created by the strong community link was not the case in the ethnic Chinese community. Surviving in the same market made Chinese restaurant owners isolate themselves both physically and socially from each other. Thus, the Chinese were not only geographically divided but also socially divided with a lack of social cohesion. The social network size within the Chinese community was very small (Rochelle and Shardlow, 2013). The difficulty to connect within the community was largely due to the reason that most of them worked in the same restaurant sector.

The Chinese community in Britain is not homogeneous. It is made up of members from diverse origins with different cultural backgrounds and different languages being spoken. There are three main groups: people from most parts of China who speak Mandarin, people from Hong Kong and Guangdong province (a province in Southern China) who speak Cantonese and British-born Chinese (BBC), for whom English is their first language.

Because the first group of Chinese immigrants was from Hong Kong, Chinese businesses and organisations in the early days were established by Hong Kong people who spoke Cantonese. Discussions above have indicated that the UK's Chinese community has recently moved into a society where the population from mainland China was the major constitution. Cantonese was regarded as the problem in communication by many mainland Chinese who spoke Mandarin. Significant problems emerged between the two groups of people with different languages being spoken. In Chan et al. (2007)'s research, there were examples to reveal the conflict. A respondent from Cardiff explained:

> People from the Cardiff Chinese Christian Church asked me to join their activities several times. Because they are Hong Kong people, we found it difficult to talk with them.
>
> (Chan et al., 2007, pp. 521)

Another said:

> Unfortunately, Chinese people here are mainly from Guangdong and Hong Kong. It is difficult for me to understand them. People from Cardiff Chinese Christian Church are mainly Hong Kong people. The

church has set up a Chinese school where Cantonese is taught. Our children don't go there because they can't understand.

(Chan et al., 2007, pp. 521)

Due to the language barrier, there had been little communication between Cantonese speakers and Mandarin speakers. People identified themselves largely based on the languages being spoken and regions they were originally from. The language issue, as a result, created social division between the two groups of people.

British-born Chinese also viewed themselves as a distinct group. BBC was one of the fastest growing groups in the UK. For the second generation of Hong Kong Chinese only, there was an annual growth of 9.9% from 2001 to 2007 (Rochelle and Shardlow, 2013). Most viewed themselves more as British, with only ethnic connection to China. They established their communities and organisations for discussions and sharing ideas. Moreover, as mainland Chinese immigrants generally did not have a decent English language skill, this also caused communication problems within the community.

Thus, with different traditions, different language being spoken and different perceptions of people from different parts of the country, there were potentially tensions between different group members.

Building the Research and the Plan of the Book

Over the past decades, existing research has explained ethno-cultural and socio-economic development within the ethnic Chinese community in Britain, which provides valuable insights into understanding this group. However, nearly all of the research had the focus at the community level; there has been little research in studying how workplace relations were influenced in ethnic Chinese businesses. Given the increasing importance of the ethnic Chinese small businesses under the UK economy and a frequent call that understanding needs to be informed by analyses of the integration of diverse minority groups, a piece of extensive research examining how workplace relations are experienced in ethnic Chinese small firms is required. The research conducted by Lee (2019) was an attempt to examine behaviours and management at workplaces with relatively more in-depth data. It discussed shop floor dynamics between owner-managers and workers in ethnic Chinese businesses in Los Angeles. However, the research cannot adequately develop the link between the context and shop floor behaviours in interpreting employment relationships, as he mentioned:

My findings indicated that business traditions and high levels of competition may contribute to informal practices, though I cannot assess the exact role of these contextual factors. Future research examining contextual factors can clarify our understandings of how and under what conditions employers engage in informal economic practices.

(Lee, 2019, pp. 447)

In addressing the research gap, this research sets to examine the nature of employment relations in ethnic Chinese small firms in the UK context. It is to explore how management practices and employment relationships are experienced in the ethnic Chinese restaurant sector within the UK context and the main factors that shape this process.

The structure of the book is listed below:

Chapter 2 is the methodology chapter. It explains the research methods used to conduct the study and justifies the research by discussing relevant methodological concerns. Additionally, the research settings are introduced in detail.

Chapter 3 discusses the product market pressures management faced in the sector. The nature of demand fluctuation will be examined. The discussion analyses how intense competition and uncertainties caused by the turbulent environment influenced labour control strategies and employment relationships.

Chapter 4 explores how the labour market affected the shop floor dynamics between owner-managers and workers. Three groups of workers—chefs, kitchen assistants and front area workers—are the focus. The chapter analyses how their labour market positions and the dependence of the owners shaped the effort bargaining process.

Chapter 5 focuses on the multi-cultural workforces. It shows how workplace relations were influenced by different languages being spoken. The chapter discusses how guessing and intersubjectivity played a central role in accommodating owners and workers in the face of language barriers, and the problems arising from the process. Moreover, conflicts and struggles between members from different groups are described and explained, which had significant impacts on people's behaviours.

Chapter 6 discusses how informality interacting with ethnicity affected management practices and employment relationships. As a defining characteristic of employment relations in small firms, informality was also present in ethnic Chinese restaurants. The order was negotiated in a continuous process on the shop floor. Informality interacted with a series of external factors and internal forces in shaping different types of workplace fiddles. The chapter also analyses the extent to which shop floor behaviours were constrained by various laws and regulations. It examines how owners and workers were alleged to collaborate to breach regulations, in which different patterns of relations were formed.

Chapter 7 is the discussion chapter. The concluding chapter will review the key findings of the study. By synthesising the findings, it discusses the empirical insights, theoretical generalisation and methodological significance of the study.

2 Methodology

This study was located within a rich empirical tradition by taking ethnography as the approach. The fieldwork for the current study consisted of participant observation of restaurant work for a period of seven months spent in two ethnic Chinese restaurants in Sheffield. The in-depth data collected from the field enabled the research to interpret people's behaviours on the shop floor and develop the connection between employment relations and the context, which is the value of the research.

This chapter starts from examining the nature of the ethnographic approach and reviewing highly-influential studies to demonstrate the value of the ethnographic approach to workplace studies. The next few sections discuss key methodological concerns in ethnography and justifies the research by providing insights into the actual process in which the research was conducted. Finally, the research settings will be introduced in detail.

Ethnography as the Research Approach

Locating the Research Under the Empirical Tradition of Workplace Studies

Ethnography is the research methodology in which researchers participate in organisations, societies and people's lives for an extended period of time to collect data for their studies (Hammersley and Atkinson, 1995). It normally involves direct participation in and observation of the settings they are studying. Hammersley and Atkinson emphasised that the nature of ethnography is rooted in the philosophy of interpretivism and social constructivism. The ethnographic approach acknowledges the interaction between actors and the contexts, rejecting a universal truth and objective reality. The social meanings of individuals' perceptions and behaviours are constructed within the contexts. Thus, ethnography explains human actions and generates explanations based on the rich data collected in the field.

There has been a rich empirical tradition in studying workplace relations (Roy, 1952, 1954; Lupton, 1963; Burawoy, 1979; Edwards and Scullion, 1982; Scott, 1994; Ram, 1994). These studies provided intensive examinations of management–worker relations based on the ethnographic approach. By employing participant observation and ethnography as the research approach, researchers directly engaged in workplaces, which enabled them to gain an in-depth understanding of the context and explain the nature of shop floor behaviours. The ethnographic approach gave researchers the opportunity to study the context in a natural setting to examine the complexity and heterogeneity of workplace relations and explain the meanings and significances between people and the environment. Theories and insights generated from these studies such as effort bargaining, shop floor accommodation, workplace fiddles and management resistance had significant impacts upon how empirical understandings and conceptual ideas were developed in later research. The value of the ethnographic approach into workplace studies can reach a degree other research techniques cannot achieve.

In the field of employment relations in small firms particularly, it is suggested that research in studying the processes of management required insights informed by direct observations from the shop floor (Ram, 1996). Building on a methodological review, Ram and Edwards (2010) summarised:

> Many of these studies have adopted a case study approach or other intensive methods of investigation. This has been fundamental to elucidating the lived experience of employment relations in small firms and the subtle forms of control at play in such settings.
>
> (Ram and Edwards, 2010, pp. 241)

Moreover, Chan et al. (2007) identified that most of the existing work in researching the UK Chinese communities relevant to workplace studies used survey and questionnaire as the research methods. There has been a lack of in-depth research to explore the dynamics between owners and workers at the point of production.

Given the importance of the empirical tradition in exploring workplace relations, the nature of the study and the current research gap, ethnography was employed as the approach. The research echoes the view that the social meaning of people's behaviour and shop floor experiences may be significantly different within different contexts (Curran and Stanworth, 1979; Ram, 1994). The study acknowledges that it is a series of interactive processes between humans and particular contexts. The structural settings have been taken into account to construct the analysis to interpret people's behaviour. As a piece of exploratory research, it follows the nature of ethnography used in social science – unravelling and revealing the relationships and meanings of between actors and the environments.

Gold (1958) classified four types of field roles in the ethnographic approach. Ethical considerations ruled out the two covert roles for this research. The 'participant-as-observer' is the role where 'the researcher engages in regular interaction with people and participants in their daily lives and members of the social setting are aware of the researcher's status as a researcher' (Bryman and Bell, 2007, pp. 454). The discussion above has demonstrated how directly engaging in the field can enable researchers to generate an in-depth understanding of behaviours on the shop floor. With this reason, the study took the 'participant-as-observer' role to conduct the fieldwork.

Generalisation

Ethnographic studies are often criticised with the claim that their findings are not generalisable to wider contexts and populations because of their small number of cases (Steinmetz, 2004; Gerring, 2007). When it comes to the criteria for assessing the rigour of research, ethnography is believed to have a low level of 'reliability' and 'population validity' (Capelli, 1985).

It was argued that the criticism was mistaken and based upon a partial understanding of what it means to 'generalise' from a particular case to the wider situations. Mitchell (1983), for example, explained that criticisms pointed at the limited population validity of ethnographic data confuse research techniques which are appropriate to quantitative research with those involved in qualitative research. The generalisation from ethnographic findings does not suggest the representativeness of events but relies on the strength of the analysis. Ethnographic research does not aim to demonstrate how common a particular phenomenon is, but rather to explore and explain why situations work in the way they do (Hammersley, 1998). Yin (2009) also noted that ethnography is to discuss analytical generalisation. It is not an approach that focuses on empirical or quantitative generalisation. The approach of ethnography is aiming to examine the principles in a particular environment to develop conceptual and theoretical generalisation based on empirical data (Tsang, 2014). For example, Burawoy (1979) illustrated how capitalist social relations are reproduced over time in the form of consent. Ram (1994) demonstrated that the relationship between owner-managers and workers was largely shaped by informal negotiation in small firms, which challenged the structure-determinism view.

As mentioned above, this research took a 'participant-as-observer' role, where participants were aware of my identity as a researcher. Although I had specific jobs during my fieldwork, I had the freedom to observe people's behaviours, contact with workers and ask questions around the issues that might be related to my research, which provided robust evidence in explaining participants' behaviours and the context, reflecting consistency in the process of data collection. Additionally, as the research took place in a period of seven months, it also had the characteristic of high levels of quantity in assuring the data were comprehensive and rich enough. This further enhances 'reliability' in the data collection process.

As a piece of exploratory research, the goal is not to conduct a numerical generalisation by examining whether the data in these two case study firms are representative and indicating how common these features are. Empirical data collected in the two restaurants were analysed in a way to develop insights in explaining the environment and shop floor behaviours and to generate theoretical understandings in a wider context. By synthesising the findings, the research developed the concept of 'ethnic twist' that denotes the conflict between co-ethnic workers with different origins (see Chapter 5 for details). Workplace behaviours and shop floor dynamics were massively influenced by the struggle and hostility between different group members. An existing framework that does not identify this concept cannot adequately explain management practices and employment relationships in ethnic Chinese small firms. A revised framework incorporating the theme not only can capture the mechanism in this context but also guide empirical research to discover different patterns of employment relations in other contexts.

Reflexivity

Reflexivity suggests that ethnographers should be aware of their social positions in the field and how they affect the data. As ethnography believes that it is impossible to separate people's values from the social world, researchers would observe the field from a particular point of view structured by the socio-economic-political environment he has experienced. When engaging in the field, their perceptions and behaviours are expected to have various implications for participants. For these reasons, researchers are required to critically reflect on their field experiences and to understand their roles in affecting the behaviours of others (Gill and Johnson, 2002). It is impossible to avoid researcher-as-participant influence, but it is necessary for a researcher to be always aware of their potential impacts (Hammersley and Atkinson, 1995).

There would have been strong negative impacts upon the findings without realising the importance of 'reflectivity' in my research. As already mentioned in Chapter 2, there were typically three different groups of workers in the ethnic Chinese community. Chapter 5 illustrated that explicit conflicts existed between Mandarin speaking workers and Cantonese speaking workers. I am a Mandarin speaker. Having worked in the field for a period, workers with the Mandarin background sometimes would like me together with them to engage struggle toward Cantonese workers' control. They gradually treated me largely as a member of the Mandarin union, not exactly a researcher. That was obviously because of my Mandarin background and more frequent contacts with Mandarin workers. Under these circumstances, my perception was also influenced to some extent by my feeling that the Cantonese workers were to be blamed for weakening the solidarity. I soon realised I had to keep a balanced view towards these two groups without being affected by their struggles, and meanwhile, I managed to minimise the influence of my cultural background by clearly stating my position as a researcher.

The example also denotes that being immersed in the field for a long time, especially as a fully functioning member, ethnographers may lose their sense of being a researcher. They sometimes have to make decisions whether or not to support a person, a policy or to take sides (Bryman and Bell, 2007). During my fieldwork, I also experienced things like potential participation of workplace fiddles and law breaches. Once I had trapped into these kinds of situations, the data and analysis would have been hugely suspected. With the acknowledgement of my influences, I had been careful to reduce the effects on the environment and participants' behaviours throughout the study.

Choosing the Research Settings

The analysis of employment relations in small firms should benefit from the 'firm-in-sector' approach (Arrowsmith et al., 2003). Ram et al. (2000) explained that their choice of the restaurant sector was deliberate as the sector was heavily occupied by ethnic minority groups and was significantly affected by cultural influences. Earlier analysis has mentioned that there had been a tradition for ethnic Chinese to engage in the restaurant sector. This was mainly shaped by both their cultural tradition and economic positions. The catering industry accounted for an extremely high percentage of all small businesses. Thus, based on a 'firm-in-sector' view and the particular significance of the restaurant sector to the Chinese group, it is sensible to choose this sector to explore the employment relations.

Once the sector was fixed, it was time to deal with how many cases should be chosen and to what extent they should differ from each other. Edwards (1995, pp. 51) suggested that 'two or more cases can be analysed so that the causes of differences, and hence the conditions promoting one outcome rather than another, can be assessed'. A comparative study examining various cases within the tradition of ethnography can draw on the similarities and differences among different contexts to increase the power of analysis (Lupton, 1963; Edwards and Scullion, 1982). In the field of employment relations in small firms, there was obvious variation in management strategies between high-end restaurants and low-end restaurants according to their different product market and labour market positions (Jones et al., 2006). With these reasons, the research chose one up-market restaurant and one down-market restaurant as the research sites. By drawing on the comparative approach, discussions were expected to explain why some behaviour existed in one workplace instead of the other. The study, therefore, could examine the complexity and heterogeneity of workplace relations in the sector.

For contents in this book, the up-market restaurant is labelled as 'Firm U', while the down-market restaurant is labelled as 'Firm D'.

Gaining and Sustaining Access

Gaining access is one of the most important steps in organisational studies for ethnographic research. Researchers aim to get consent to allow them to study in the field. The negotiation of access includes not only securing the initial physical access but also ensuring continued access by establishing relationships with participants. Gaining permission to enter an organisation sometimes relies on researchers' resources; sustaining access requires ongoing consent by participants throughout the field work (Hammersley and Atkinson, 1995).

Gaining Initial Access

FIRM D

Securing access to Firm D was largely based on my close relationship with the manager, Jack. Jack had been working in Firm D since I came to Sheffield in January 2011. Because I was a regular customer of Firm D, we later knew each other very well. Whenever I went to eat, we would have a pleasant chat.

When the research strategy was first formulated in January 2014, I immediately considered Firm D as the potential choice for the down-market restaurant because it had been one of the busiest restaurants in Sheffield. I then went to meet Jack and expressed my desire to be a waiter for a period of time. Jack responded positively. He agreed to allow me to conduct my research once my plan was fixed. Finding a job there, as he promised to me, would not be a problem.

In November 2014, when the research was well planned, I found Jack telling him I was ready to work. He asked me how long I could work. I told him it was probably about two or three months. He thought this would cause some difficulties because the owner would like to recruit a long-term waiter. I then recalled the technique used by Holliday (see Ram and Holliday, 1993). She successfully secured access by using the technique called 'bargaining cards', where a researcher exchanged the permission of access by offering some practical benefits to the business. In her case, she worked as a free worker to 'buy' the access, which would otherwise earn her approximately £2,500. In exchange for the access, I asked Jack to tell the owner that I would be happy to earn half of the wages. On that evening, he texted me saying that the owner agreed to meet me at 11 AM the next day. I arrived at Firm D the next day at 11 AM and subsequently did a three-hour trial as the owner required. After that, the owner agreed to offer me the job with half pay.

FIRM U

Gaining initial access in Firm U was also largely based on direct communication. It was a Sunday afternoon when I first went into Firm U. I asked the front area manager whether they were in need of any front area staff. She told me that they did not require any service staff at the moment. However, they needed someone working in the kitchen area. She asked me to come back again at 10 PM because the owner would be there around that time so that I could speak to the owner directly.

I met the owner in the evening. After a few words, the owner quickly identified that I was from Beijing, adjacent to Tianjin municipality where he came from, both in the north of China. It felt obvious that this created a close feeling between us at the start. The owner confirmed that he did need kitchen staff. Although I expressed the doubt that I might be not capable enough to take a kitchen assistant job, the owner seemed to feel strongly confident about me. He later offered me the kitchen assistant job without even requiring a trial. The access was successfully secured in an unanticipated way.

One thing that has to be highlighted is that, except for an initial introduction to the research from me, the owner asked nothing about my research. He had no interests at all in my study. It felt that it was urgent for him to recruit me to fill the vacancy to keep the business running, although I knew nothing about cooking in a restaurant. Later on, after being in the field for a while, I knew that the reason why he recruited me was that two out of three chefs were planning to leave at that moment. Due to the shortage in the labour market, the owner could not find any proper kitchen assistant immediately. I was just the one who applied for a job at that particular time. That is why I could quickly secure the access, genuinely having no relationship with my background and my research.

Maintaining and Sustaining Access

The last section explained how the initial access was secured in the two firms. Indeed, sustaining access was not an easy task. Below shows how I sustained my access in the two case study firms.

FIRM D

Figure 2.1 shows the process of maintaining access in Firm D. The ongoing process of maintaining access was continuous over time. With a reasonable input of negotiation on access, it gave access to a large portion of data. It followed 'the 80/20 rule'—with more time and input spent in the field, a researcher got higher trust and more access (Gummesson, 2000). Sustaining research access was a cumulative process in Firm D. I did not encounter substantial crisis during the period of fieldwork. I got on well with most of the employees, although the cultural differences between groups of workers had some negative influences (further analysis in Chapter 5). Additionally, receiving half pay gave me the advantage over

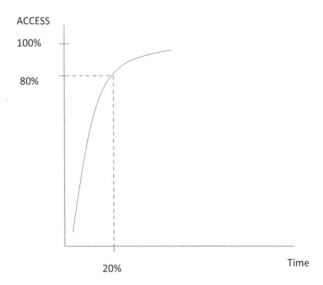

Figure 2.1 The Process of Maintaining Access in Firm D

other front area workers given that the nature of the work did not require special ability.

However, maintaining access in Firm U created a few problems. Figure 2.2 shows this process.

It consists of four stages. First, it started from gaining initial access. This was conducted by direct communication with the owner-manager, which was achieved by successfully gaining a job. At this stage, it was mainly concerned with building trust with the owner. Once the initial access was secured, the next stage was to develop access with the staff. Because the owner rarely appeared on the site, what I mainly focused on here was to build trust and relationships with employees. It then moved into the third stage—the turbulent stage. Due to the management-worker conflicts and the influences from the external environment, the business experienced a huge staff turnover. Additionally, Firm U had a three-week refurbishment during that period. After the refurbishment, workers were almost completely changed. With the significant staff turnover, the level of access dropped considerably. At stage 4, I had to re-develop relationships with new workers from scratch, as I did at stage 2. The challenge at this stage was to build trust with them.

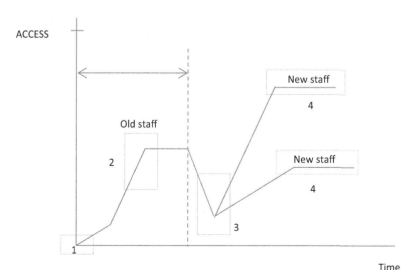

Figure 2.2 The Process of Maintaining Access in Firm U

After examining the entire process of gaining and sustaining access, it was apparent that negotiating access in Firm U fluctuated significantly. Under this environment, successfully sustaining research access was far more complicated than the 'accumulative model' as achieved in Firm D. Reduction existed throughout the process. It meant that access could not always be continuous and constant. This discontinuous process was largely attributed to the firm's particular business position in a turbulent environment (further analysis in Chapter 3) and the negative influences from the conflicts between Northern and Southern people due to different languages, cultures and traditions (further analysis in Chapter5).

The specific working periods were: the intensive fieldwork in Firm D was from 23rd November 2014 to 14th March 2015; the intensive fieldwork in Firm U was from 29th March 2015 to 4th July 2015.

Introducing the Firms

Firm D

Firm D was founded in 2007, and at that time was one of the very few Chinese restaurants located in the university area. In 2011, it moved to a larger property next door due to continuously increased customers. The main service of Firm D was rice served with meat and vegetables and noodle soups. The average price for each dish was £6.50. The food amount was sufficient for a normal person for a meal. Additionally, it also provided stir-fry dishes and a few dishes for non-Chinese. The owners of Firm D were a couple, both from Hong Kong. The female owner worked in the front area as a full-time waitress, while the male owner worked in the kitchen as the head chef.

The physical location was the biggest advantage of Firm D. Its location was near the University of Sheffield and the Sheffield International College, which provided the fundamental customer base. Moreover, the university area was also the area where most Chinese students lived. Thus, the physical location won Firm D a considerable number of regular customers. An ideal geographical location had enabled it to become one of the busiest Chinese restaurants in Sheffield.

Apart from its geographical advantage, Firm D also relied on its variety of dishes to attract customers. It had more than 100 selections of rice served with meat and vegetables and noodle soups. No other restaurants provided as many choices as Firm D did. By contrast, its choices of stir-fry dishes were limited. It did not even have a stir-fry dish menu before 2014. The strategy of Firm D was to fully satisfy the customers who had needs for cheap and simple meals.

Among all the customers, less than 10% was non-Chinese. Most non-Chinese customers were university staff and students. They typically had lunch there and then went back to continue their afternoon's work. There were also a small number of regular non-Chinese customers living nearby. For Firm D's Chinese customers, over 90% of them were students from the University of Sheffield and the Sheffield International College. Its customers could be generally divided into two groups: lunchtime customers on weekdays, and dinner time and weekend customers.

Lunch shifts in Firm D were from 11 AM to 3 PM. There were two periods of busy time on a typical weekday at lunchtime: 12 PM to 12:40 PM and 1 PM to 1:40 PM. For the first period, customers were mainly students who were going to take their afternoon's classes. For the second period, customers were largely comprised of students who already finished their morning classes. Additionally, for each period, there were also a number of students who took a break between morning and afternoon classes. As mentioned earlier, because Firm D was near the two organisations and most of the students lived near Firm D, if they chose not to eat at home, Firm D would be a potential choice.

Students who had dinners on weekdays or meals at weekends represented another group. First, there was less pressure when it was in the evening compared to time constraints during lunchtime. Second, for those who lived far from the university area, especially for those who only had limited hours of break between morning classes and afternoon classes, it was unlikely that they had time to go home to cook and come back to continue their classes. However, when they finished their afternoon studies, there was no need for them to necessarily choose a restaurant near the university. Similarly, choices were less constrained on weekends. Most customers who had dinners on weekdays and meals on weekends ordered more expensive stir-fry dishes, instead of cheap and simple food. For students who regularly had meals at both of these periods, they were either living near Firm D or particularly fancying Firm D's food.

In term time, during lunchtime on a typical weekday, it sold at least £1,000–£1,200; at dinner time, it normally generated an income of £500. On weekends, it generally earned less than £1,000 for an entire day. This reflected that the main customers of Firm D were students who had lunch on weekdays. The high income was achieved by both its geographical advantage and its strategy on the types of dishes it provided.

Firm U

Firm U was founded in 2013. It located in what is traditionally considered Sheffield's 'China Town' area. As an up-market restaurant, Firm U mainly served the hot pot and skewer buffets. Moreover, Firm U also ran a karaoke business on the upper floor. At the beginning of 2015, to enhance its competence with continuously increased pressures coming from the product market and inferior physical location, it introduced the Korean barbecue as a supplement. There were two owners in Firm U. The female owner was previously a Master's student at the University of Manchester, while the male owner had been a chef before he earned enough money to start his first business in Manchester. They knew each other during the period when the female owner did her Master's degree, and they later founded this restaurant.

As an up-market restaurant, exquisite decoration and comfortable environment should be basic requirements. These were done very well by Firm U. Its top was well decorated by a suspended ceiling, which was rarely found among all the Chinese restaurants in Sheffield. With well-selected dim lights, it created an extraordinary relaxed feeling. Tables were all made of marble, compared to wooden or even plastic ones in almost all the other Chinese restaurants. Distance between tables was spacious, and there was sufficient room for walking. Even when it was full, it never felt awkward, in contrast to most other Chinese restaurants, where customers always ate in an extremely narrow space.

Apart from the eating environment, Firm U also had the advantage of its food service. Although Firm U was not the first to provide hot pot, it was the first to operate hot pot in the form of a buffet at a reasonable price. Additionally, its skewer buffet also had a famous reputation. None of the other restaurants had as many varieties as Firm U provided. If anybody wanted to eat skewers to the full, they had no choice but to go to Firm U. All of these elements in the beginning helped Firm U to develop its regular customer base.

Firm U's customers were nearly 100% Chinese. Before the owner decided to remove stir-fry dishes and set dishes designed for the British, there had been a few non-Chinese customers. However, after it completely operated hot pot and skewers, I could hardly see any non-Chinese customers during the entire research period. Although some non-Chinese occasionally tried hot pot there for some reasons, I never recognised any who went again for the second time. As was the case in Firm D, students accounted for over 90% of all the customers. The remaining 10% was largely ethnic Chinese immigrants. The distance from Firm U to the central university area was a 30-minute walk. Due to Firm U's location and food types, it had few customers on weekdays, especially at lunchtime. Firm U's business mainly relied on customers on weekends, which also was reflected in its revenues.

During term time, Firm U's average income from Monday to Thursday was less than £500 per day; the revenue from Friday to Sunday was over

£1,200 per day. There were two shifts a day: afternoon shift from 12 PM to 4 PM and evening shift from 5 PM to 10 PM. Its income on an afternoon shift from Monday to Thursday was normally less than £100, while the revenue on an evening shift was about £400; the revenue on an afternoon shift from Friday to Sunday was less than £300, while it could generate around £1,000 revenues on an evening shift. The data revealed that the main constitution of Firm U's customers were those who had meals at dinner time, especially on weekends, which was different from Firm D's customer base.

Conclusions

This chapter discussed ethnography as the research approach. By analysing the nature of the ethnographic approach and reviewing several pieces of highly influential work, it demonstrates the importance of the approach in studying workplace relations. The analysis drew out key themes such as generalisation, reflexivity and gaining and sustaining access to reflect how the research was conducted and justify the research.

By examining the details of Firm D and Firm U, it revealed that the two restaurants were different in many aspects, such as their product market positions, customer types and locations. With the application of the comparative approach, it was expected to capture how the differences between the two restaurants affected patterns of shop floor behaviour in various ways.

Below lists the frequently mentioned characters in the research for readers to identify easily.

Firm D

Kate—the female owner
Jack—the front area manager

Firm U

Yi: the head chef
Teng: the kitchen assistant
Ming: the initial front area manager
Zha: the second front area manager

3 Influences From the Product Market

The product market is a crucial structural factor in shaping management practices and employment relationships in small firms. Rainnie (1989) suggested that small firms' control strategies were considerably constrained by the dependence of large companies. The intense competition significantly influenced labour management choices and the dynamics of workplace relations (McMahon, 1996; Jones and Ram, 2007). Additionally, it was also argued that management structure and work organisation in small firms were primarily affected by specific customer requirements (Kinnie, 1999).

This chapter examines the product market pressures management faced in Sheffield. It aims to provide an insight into how management handled the uncertainties from the product market and its significances to employment relations. Section 1 introduces the recent development of the ethnic Chinese restaurant sector in Sheffield. Section 2 and Section 3 focus on two central issues in the sector: the nature of demand fluctuation and the level of competition. The analysis is to discuss how these two factors affected management practices and employment relationships.

The Increase in Chinese Restaurants in Sheffield

Before early-2011, the ethnic Chinese restaurant sector could not be regarded as a significant business in Sheffield. There were three located in the city centre area, three located in the university area and three located in the 'China Town' area. The restaurant sector began to boom from 2011. In mid-2015 when I finished my fieldwork, there were around 15 Chinese restaurants in the university region and over eight in the 'China Town' region. Having experienced a dramatic change like this, it is necessary to understand what led to such a difference in four years.

The Demand Side—A Continuous Increase of Chinese Students

Chapter 2 mentioned that the majority of customers in these two restaurants were Chinese students. From a basic supply-demand view, a huge increase from the supply side must be dependent upon the rise from the demand side. In this case, there had to be some significant rises in the number of Chinese students to explain this result. Table 3.1 shows the number of Chinese students the University of Sheffield recruited from 2008 to 2014 (UoS, 2019).

As the figures display in the table, Sheffield did experience a considerable rise of Chinese students recently. Since 2008, there had been a yearly increase at a rate of over 20% until 2014. In 2014, the total number was five times as many as it was in 2008. Moreover, the table also explains why the year of 2011 was the start of the booming. The number in 2010 doubled compared to 2008, soaring from 838 to 1,662. New restaurant owners realised the market potential. With some time for preparation, they began to develop their businesses in 2011. A nearly 70% rise in 2012 accelerated the development. Thus, the huge increase in the number of Chinese students fundamentally contributed to the rise in the demand side.

Table 3.1 The Number of Chinese Students the University of Sheffield Recruited From 2008 to 2014

Year	Number of Chinese students	Percentage increase compared to the previous year
2008	838	
2009	1,058	27%
2010	1,662	57%
2011	2,124	28%
2012	3,544	67%
2013	4,163	20%
2014	4,152	0%

Source: UoS, 2019

The Supply Side—Savings and Entrepreneurial Motivation From Chefs

Chapter 2 mentioned that due to the historical reason, the ethnic Chinese restaurant sector in Britain was traditionally controlled by Hong Kong people. Later arrivals from Mainland China worked for them as chefs. The situation in Sheffield perfectly fit the literature in the beginning. For the nine ethnic Chinese restaurants founded before 2011, eight owners were from Hong Kong. However, the structure of the sector changed completely after mid-2011. Owners of new Chinese restaurants were largely from Guangdong province in Southern China. People from Hong Kong never made up any large percentage.

As introduced in Chapter 2, large groups of workers from Mainland China started moving into the UK in the late 1990s. Before the late 1990s, applying for a working visa was extremely complicated, and the fees to get the warranty from a business in the UK hugely expensive. In the late 1990s, the UK government changed its policy. The application process became simplified as a result. Yi, the chef in Firm U, explained why there were so many workers from Guangdong province:

> Because the first agency after the change of the policy was established in Taishan, Guangdong province. I came to the UK in 2007. You know what? I can tell you that nearly half of the population in Taishan has moved to the UK. Furthermore, after the success in Taishan, the agency also established several branches in other cities in Guangdong. Agencies developed in other provinces were far behind. That is why there are so many chefs from Guangdong. It is not just in Sheffield. It is the same case everywhere in Britain.

One day when all the employees had lunch in Firm U, I asked Yi why the buffet had not been introduced (Firm U provided hot pot and skewer buffets, while the owner would like to also introduce a general buffet). Yi told me that the owner could not find any proper chefs:

> See what Wen and Lin did. (Wen and Lin previously worked in Firm U. They both later started their restaurants in Sheffield.) They (Chefs) have been working in the UK for over ten years, saving some money. The market is promising, so many students. Why not (open their restaurants)? Once my wife finishes giving birth to my second baby, I might open a takeaway as well.
>
> You see, Wen found two partner chefs, both of whom previously worked with him in Firm A; Lin got one partner chef, who previously worked in Firm B. Five went for developing their businesses.
>
> It is not just for him to have this difficulty (the owner in Firm U). Every owner in Sheffield cannot find proper chefs immediately because those who have skills all want to start their restaurants.

Zha, Firm U's front area manager, was also at the table at the same time. He moved to England in 2006 at the age of 15. Since then, he had been working as a waiter in Sheffield's restaurant sector for nine years. He added:

> They have skills, and they now have enough money. They have been keen to have their restaurants after torture for years as a chef. This is important for them. Moreover, the market has been booming. They can earn a little more. That is an opportunity for them.

Having worked in Britain for years, chefs from Mainland China got some savings. Based on their social connections and entrepreneurial motivations, they started their businesses under the environment with huge demands. This was why the sector could develop so much from the supply side. As most chefs were from Mainland China, it also explained the structural change where the sector was no longer dominated by Hong Kong owners.

The Unstable Environment

The Nature of Demand Fluctuation

The demand for the product market in the ethnic Chinese restaurant sector fluctuated significantly over a year's time. The owner of Firm D once vividly described the change of demands:

> Well, just to see how many students there are in (university) libraries. We are the same as them. If they have lots of students, the business is satisfying; if there are few students in the library, then the business is poor.

This indeed concisely indicated the nature of the demand fluctuation. As Firm D and Firm U both heavily relied on student customers, once the student number changed at a particular time, the demand of the two businesses would immediately follow that change. The description above actually built a relationship between the number of students and the business conditions. The student number changed dramatically in different periods based on the university semester time, which determined the demand for ethnic Chinese restaurants in the same period.

Figure 3.1 roughly describes the demand fluctuation in the ethnic Chinese restaurant sector over a year's time.

This diagram starts in August. Undergraduate students by August have finished their studies and left the UK. With the decrease of undergraduate students, the average demand drops correspondingly. As a result, demands in August are at a relatively low level. The university semester starts in late September. With the arrival of new students, the demand begins to rise in September. For the next three months, the demand is stable at a high level. The first significant drop occurs in mid-December. It is the end of the first semester and the start of the Christmas holiday. During the Christmas vacation, most Chinese students are either back to China or travelling around. The ethnic Chinese restaurant sector experiences the worst period in a year. Once the Christmas vacation ends and the second semester starts, the average demand goes back to a high level in mid-January. It then falls to another

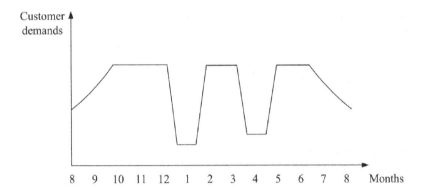

Figure 3.1 The Demand Fluctuation in the Ethnic Chinese Restaurant Sector

low level during the Easter vacation starting from late March. After the holiday, the demand will again return to a relatively high level until mid-June. Finally, from mid-June to August, there is more turbulence in student numbers due to the end of the second semester and the departure of the students who already graduated, which leads to low demands.

The actual revenues that the two restaurants generated followed the model. In Firm D, for a typical day in November, its income at lunchtime was generally between £1,000 and £1,200; average income at dinner time was £400–£600. By contrast, during the Christmas and Easter vacations, its average lunchtime revenue was less than £400, and dinner time revenue was around £200. Jack, the manager in Firm D, explained:

> We have the least customers at Christmas. During Easter, the Summer School students from China and Singapore can contribute to some businesses. During the Christmas vacation, an entire day revenue is only some hundred pounds.

On a day in early January 2015, when it was during the low demand period, I had a discussion with Kate, the owner of Firm D, about the situation. She said:

> It will get a bit better at the end of this month. However, the poor condition will last for another couple of weeks. We have to endure this. There are no other ways to turn around.

When I did my fieldwork in Firm U, I also had a discussion with Wen about Firm U's business conditions at different periods. He told me:

Look, I came here on 17th August 2014. The revenue for the first week was £2,800. The second week, £2,900; the third week, £3,600; the fourth week, over £5,000. Since then, it had been generally around £5,000 a week till Christmas. The top weekly revenue it generated was £8,000 in mid-October. At the first week of November, it was £7,800. During the Christmas period, the average weekly revenue was around £3,000.

It was during the Easter vacation when I started my fieldwork in Firm U. Weekly revenues during that period were around £3,000. However, when the Easter vacation had already ended, the weekly revenue soon rose to an average of £5,000 per week.

Up to this point, I already described the fluctuation of customer demands over different periods of a year time. The specific figures from the two restaurants exactly fit this model. The next section will focus on constraints caused by the unstable market on owner-managers' choices in labour management and its meanings to employment relations.

Owner-Managers' Choices Under the Unstable Product Environment and Implications to Employment Relations

Running a business in such a context, the most affected aspects of owner-managers' labour management practices were staff recruitment and dismissal. As shown above, the demand fluctuation was frequent. The actual recruitment and dismissal practices in the two restaurants exactly followed the demand change. Owner-managers recruited new employees in advance to face high demand periods and dismissed labour before the business went into low demand periods.

The first time when I negotiated the access of Firm D was in mid-June 2014. Jack told me that summer vacation was underway so that there were few customers. As a result, the owner did not plan to recruit any front area workers. At that time, two were enough to provide the service. He worked on the lunch shift, while Kate, the owner, worked on the evening shift. Later, in early September, the owner posted a recruitment note on the window. As Figure 3.1 shows, it was the time when businesses were going to experience the high demand period.

When I started to work in Firm D in late November 2014, the number of front area workers was already up to four on both lunch shifts and dinner shifts, compared to one on each shift during the summer time. The four-employee structure lasted for several weeks. In the first week of the Christmas vacation, when the roster was released, I became the only part-time worker. In the final week of the Christmas vacation, Kate began to contact former part-time workers. The number was back to four on each shift in the first week of the second term.

In Firm U, frequent recruitment and dismissal basically took place in the same way following the demand change. After the refurbishment, there were only three working in the kitchen area, including me. The owner soon recruited a pot-washer and a kitchen assistant as it was during the high customer demand period. When it went into June, the revenue began to drop. The owner came to the site in mid-June and had a short talk with the newly recruited kitchen assistant. I later asked the kitchen assistant what the owner had said to her. She replied:

> He gave me the slip with his phone number. He said: We have very few customers now. You go to take a two-week break. When your vacation ends, just call me if you would like to come back.

She was then dismissed completely due to the decrease of customers after working in Firm U for less than three weeks.

For front area employees, there had been two on lunch shifts on weekdays for the first two weeks since Firm U re-opened. On the first day of the third week, I found that there was only Zha, the front area manager, working there. I asked him the reason. He said:

> He (the owner) asked me to remove part-time workers on lunch shifts on weekdays because customers started to drop from June.

Apart from staff recruitment and dismissal, owners in the two restaurants also had similar selection criteria under a product market environment like this. For my case, I immediately secured my employment in Firm D after a three-hour trial. Chapter 2 mentioned that the 'half wage' technique facilitated the negotiation process. Another important reason was that I could get the work done fast. Jack explained this to me after Kate had decided to recruit me:

> In the trial period, the only concern for her is your speed. Whether you can finish these tasks quickly is crucial. She will teach you other jobs afterwards.

During my research in Firm D, two candidates were immediately considered to have failed the trial due to a low working pace.

In Firm U, the owner largely used the same standard to measure. After the refurbishment, there were only three working in the kitchen—me as a kitchen assistant and two chefs, Yi and Dong. Yi told me that the owner would recruit another kitchen assistant soon. One day when I arrived, someone was working there. After a few chats, the man told me that he had come to do a trial. About 30 minutes later, Yi had some words with him. He then packed his bag and left. I asked Yi what had happened. Yi told me:

> The owner phoned me just now, asking me how his trial went on. I told him that he was fine. The only problem is that his pace is a little slow. He immediately asked me to let him go.

If recruitment and dismissal practices would ideally adapt to the change of customer demands, it was expected that owners could fully handle the uncertainty. However, the actual adaptation could not always fit the demand fluctuation model. The frequent demand change led to two types of management problems: employee dismissal before the transition from a high demand period to a low demand period (early adjustment) and employee recruitment after the transition from a low demand period to a high demand period (late adjustment).

Gui was a part-time kitchen assistant in Firm D; she only worked on lunch shifts. Before the Christmas vacation in 2014, she was told to take a break during Christmas due to low demands. In the first week after the vacation, the owner did not call her back although customers rose back to a high level immediately. One day it was really busy for serving eat-in customers, and there were also several takeaway orders. The task of delivering takeaways was normally conducted by Huo, another kitchen assistant in Firm D. However, Huo was too busy to deliver. Only Jack and I worked in the front area at that time. Jack complained to me:

> I do not know why she (Kate, the owner) has not called back Gui. There have been lots of customers since the end of the vacation. Shit!

He then phoned Kate; Kate said she would come to deliver the takeaways. Later that day, Kate asked Gui to come to work the next week.

When I started my fieldwork in Firm U in late March 2015, there were only three in the kitchen: two chefs and one kitchen assistant. One day, after a discussion about the intensity of their work, the head chef complained:

> You know what? We have been like this for over a month. I have not even taken a day off for two weeks running. The owner sacked one pot washer and one kitchen assistant in early March. He believed there would be few customers during the Easter vacation. Yes, it is, but the drop is not as quick as he thought. He should at least have left one for us. I am now washing plates every day. Are you kidding? Have you ever heard of any head chef washing plates?

In June 2015, the owner in Firm U reduced the number of lunch shift employees in the front area from two down to one. One day after the adjustment, the owner went to inspect the restaurant. He had some words with Zha and Yi and left. Zha, the front area manager, looked frustrated. I asked him the reason. He explained:

> He (the owner) walked around the dining area and indicated several problems. For example, the area surrounding the counter was not clean, tables were greasy, and the toilets smelled unpleasant. Damn it! He asked me not to use part-time workers on day shifts. How can I finish all of these things by myself? If it was in July or August, that would be fine. However, there are still many customers now. I need to serve them. If he always behaves like this, I am leaving. Shit!

These examples demonstrated that management adaptation could not adequately match the demand fluctuation. There were always fewer workers than it actually needed. According to Zha's words, labour costs accounted for one-third of total income in this sector. Whether it was 'early adjustment' or 'late adjustment', it seemed to be a rational decision from the owners to control labour costs. However, the cost control strategy under the turbulent market often caused dilemmas to employees. Yi once said to me:

> Sometimes, you think it (a large amount of work) cannot be completed, but the owner believes it can be done. You've got to do it.

Workers had to work heavily to sort out the problem caused by owners' failure to make a proper adjustment in recruitment and dismissal. Due to the lack of employees on the shop floor, the ways of management were also affected. Owner-managers generally took harsh control in managing labour, especially during high demand periods, which exerted significant pressures upon employees.

In Firm D, one service requirement was that if a customer did not order any drink, a waiter needed to provide a cup of tap water for him after ordering. On a Saturday evening, only Kate and I were on that shift. Kate mainly took orders and checked bills at the counter while I served the customers. The restaurant was full that evening so that I did not even have one second to take a rest. I had to keep delivering dishes, cleaning tables and placing fresh sets. Having temporarily finished her work, Kate found that I did not provide tap water to a few customers. She shouted at me:

> Water! Water! Lewis, water! Come to give them water!

I immediately went to the counter to prepare water and explained to her that it was too busy. However, she seemed to be unaware of the extremely busy environment and the fact that I was the only waiter. She continued to shout:

> Hurry up! Send the water to them!

As all Firm D's nearly 20 tables of customers were served by me, even if my working pace was higher than average, it was arguably inevitable that certain tasks would lag behind. However, the owner just kept pushing me without taking the specific situation into account.

On-the-job training had been the method used in Firm D to save cost. Han started her job on 19th January 2015, the day when the second semester began. She only did a three-hour trial previously. Due to the lack of practice, Han could not react quickly to customer demands. Three weeks later, she was sacked by the owner. During her three weeks of working, she was frequently criticised by Kate in an autocratic manner:

> You need to lead them on a table for two, not a table for four! It is lunchtime. We are extremely busy.
> Chopsticks! Chopsticks! They are not Chinese. You need to ask them whether they can use chopsticks.
> Be quick! Be quick! Come to deliver dishes.
> How come you have not remembered the serving procedures for hot pot? You have been here for so long.

As mentioned in Chapter 2, Firm U's owner rarely came to the site because he owned two other restaurants in Manchester. Management was largely controlled by Zha, the front area manager, and Yi, the head chef. Orders were passed down to them from the owner by phone. It was a Saturday evening in June 2015; the owner came to the site to take money. When a waitress gave me an order sheet, I found that there were numbers on the sheet, instead of straightforward dish names. Although one number matched one dish in the menu, nobody had ever written numbers because if waiters wrote numbers, kitchen workers had to read the menu to find out which number referred to which dish, which cost a lot of time. I then asked the waitress not to write numbers next time. The owner heard our talk and went in immediately, speaking to me angrily:

> It's me that asked her to use numbers. There is a table of non-Chinese. They cannot understand Chinese. We've got only two front area staff. One is cleaning, and the other is serving. They don't have time to

translate English into Chinese. Writing numbers is convenient for them. You need to check these numbers from the menu. Starting from today, we begin to use numbers!

Due to 'early adjustment', there were only two front area workers, although it had not yet transitioned from the high demand period into the low demand period. Because the limited number of workers could not handle customer demands quickly, the owner changed the method in order to improve the ordering efficiency. In this case, the tremendous pressures experienced by front area employees were passed down to kitchen workers.

In the face of the market fluctuation, owner-managers had to frequently recruit and dismiss employees to match the change. With a considerable concern for controlling the labour costs, the adaptation could not always ideally follow the demand change, which caused two types of management problems. Whether it was staff dismissal before the transition from a high demand period to a low demand period or staff recruitment after the transition from a low demand period to a high demand period, the result was that there had been fewer workers than actually needed. This also explained why speed was the key measurement in selection. However, the problems arising from the management accommodation created huge pressures on workers. Once they could not work fast or perform effectively, tensions and conflicts would occur between the two parties and subsequently influence their employment relationships.

Competition and Market Positions

The Level of Competition

Firm C was a higher-end Chinese restaurant located in the city centre area and founded in 2008. Zha, the front area manager in Firm U, worked there from 2009 to 2013. One day, we discussed the competitive market in Sheffield, he spoke to me:

> I started to work in Firm C in 2009. In 2009, it was always full on an evening shift. In 2010, the table turnover rate on a dinner shift was two. In 2011, it was three. In 2012, the number dropped a little bit. In 2013 when I left, it was less than two.

I said:

> You know what? I went there last Saturday. There were only four or five tables of customers. It was on Saturday!

Zha continued:

> It has been like this for a long time. Look, see how many restaurants have opened since 2011 in the university area (Zha then started to calculate the number of restaurants). There are now at least 15 now. Suppose each of them only attracts one table of customers. How many are there altogether?

I also asked similar questions to Jack about the level of competition. Jack told me:

> The sector cannot be compared to several years ago. The peak time was 2011 and 2012. That is why it moved here at that time (In September 2011, Firm D moved to a much larger property next door). During that period, the average revenue on lunch shifts (in Firm D) was around £2,000. The table turnover rate was at least two. Now, it is hardly full.

One day when I was chatting with Yi, I suggested he open a restaurant. He answered:

> No, I won't. It is already over saturated. There is no business at all. The meat (customers) is limited, too many restaurants.

'What if dishes are extremely delicious and dedicated, and there is a good marketing strategy?' I asked him. Yi replied:

> No, these are not important at all. The fundamental problem is that the competition is too intense. It is over-supplied. Currently, if a business can generate £10,000 revenue a week, that would be good. Previously it was £30,000 (per week).

This chapter in the beginning discussed a recent development of the ethnic Chinese restaurant sector in Sheffield. The sector started to boost from 2011 due to the increase in Chinese students. Although the student number stopped growing from 2014, this did not prevent the sector from expanding. Take the university area as an example; Chinese restaurants rose from three in 2011 to more than 15 in 2015. This sector finally went into saturation and over-supply, as described by Jack, Zha and Yi.

Having discussed the competitive environment, the next sections will analyse the significance of high levels of competition on the exercise of strategic choices by owner-managers in this context.

Pricing Strategies

As mentioned above, Firm U had a refurbishment during my fieldwork. Before the refurbishment, the price was £12.99 per person for the hot pot and skewer buffet. After the re-decoration, the owner changed the pricing strategy: £12.99 on weekdays and £16.99 at weekends (including Friday evenings).

A week after the price went up, the revenue was less than £800 on Saturday, compared to £1,200 previously at weekends. Yi began to complain:

> If he does not change the price, there will be fewer customers. Yesterday, I asked Zha to get feedback from customers. They all expressed that it was too expensive.

Zha was with us and confirmed this. Yi continued:

> All the restaurants operating hot pot buffets in Sheffield sell at the price of £13.99 or £14.99. He (the owner) sells it at fucking £16.99! Is there any gold in the meal? Yesterday, Zha told me that current customers were all our regular customers. Once they finish eating this time, it is impossible for them to come back.
>
> You know what? Firm D once did refurbishment two years ago. After that, it raised its dish prices ranging from 50 pence to £1. Customers immediately disappeared. It then turned the price back within a month.

In the third week, the revenue on Saturday dropped below £400. The owner came to the site on the fourth week and set the price back to £12.99.

I also had some discussions with Jack about possible strategies an owner could take in the face of intense competition. Jack told me:

> It is purely dog-eat-dog. In order to attract customers, Firm F (a restaurant opening in early-2015) took the 50% return strategy. If you spent £20, they gave you a £10 voucher. It was utterly ridiculous. You know what? The total cost including everything for a £7 dish is £5. They sold at half price.
>
> They chose to conduct the strategy at the beginning of the university semester. It lasted for a while. However, the result was that they could not generate any profits. And meanwhile, there were few customers for other restaurants. Finally, no one could earn money.

Under the environment of fierce competition, profit margins were very low. In order to gain more profits, owner-managers might choose to increase prices after improving restaurant conditions, such as refurbishment. This was indeed fair enough. However, the problem was that customers were sensitive to the price. It was proved not achievable given the failure in Firm D and Firm U. Reducing prices aiming to attract customers was another choice taken by these owners. However, because of the low profit margins, this would seriously hurt the business in that period. Once its price went up, it might face the same dilemma as Firm D and Firm U experienced.

Retaining Customers

In order to retain regular customers, Firm D introduced a 'loyalty card' in early December 2014. Indeed, the strategy had been executed months ago by Firm G, Firm D's main competitor. Firm G was founded in mid-2012, next door to Firm D. Firm D and Firm G were both down-market restaurants mainly operating on cheap lunchtime meals. They had similar dishes and the same price level. However, since the opening of Firm G, Firm D had been in a weaker position in the competition. Kate clearly understood the situation. Several times, she asked me to take a look at Firm G's customer amounts, although customers in Firm G for most of the time outnumbered Firm D's. Jack summarised the key reason:

> It is because of her (Kate) management problem. She has been using the same strategy to manage the business and serve customers. A few years ago, if students did not eat here, they had no other choices. Yes, she was the boss at that time. She could dictate customers. She could serve them with no respect. Even if students were unhappy with her manner, they had no more choices. However, things have changed. It is no longer the situation when it was a few years ago. Now, they have loads of choices. If you make them unhappy, they will never come back.

According to Jack, the main disadvantage of Firm D was its poor service quality. This was indeed the major difference between these two firms based on my observation. In order to reduce labour costs, Firm D's owner employed as few employees as it could. Given the limited number of front area workers, one of the consequences was that customers had to order at the counter. This seriously influenced customer experiences, as Jack analysed:

> Well, except here, is there any other Chinese restaurant requiring the customer to order at the counter? This is the principal reason why Firm D has much fewer customers than Firm G on evening shifts. On lunch shifts, students are all busy. They only order quick meals. However,

they have time in the evening. They would like to be served well. Eating here with your ten friends means that you need first to remember the name of the ten dishes you are going to order, and then you tell her (Kate) at the counter. If somebody is ordering, you have got to stand there for five minutes to be served. It is absolutely absurd. If she employed one more, everything would be better.

Furthermore, Kate's manner in treating customers also considerably influenced the business negatively. On a lunch shift, after Kate had delivered a dish, the customer expressed that it was not the one he ordered. Kate then forced him to eat the 'wrong' dish by telling him that it was similar to what he ordered. The customer finally accepted the 'wrong' dish. Jack later told me that as this customer was a regular customer, he went to say sorry to him before he left. The customer complained that there was no way for him to eat at Firm D again. It was no doubt Kate's mistake by taking the wrong order. However, if she had asked the chef to cook the 'correct' meal, it would have caused extra costs. She just would not want this to happen.

I chatted with quite a lot of customers throughout my research in Firm D. Most of them felt that the service quality and eating experience in Firm D were unpleasant. One even told me that if he saw Kate was inside, he would turn away immediately and choose another restaurant.

In a highly competitive market, if raising prices was a problem, reducing costs would be a fair choice for owners. However, if cost reduction took place at the price of minimising service quality, a business would struggle severely. Customers could change with no transfer cost.

Moving Upward

At the beginning of this chapter, it has mentioned that there were two principal reasons for the increase in the supply side: enough savings from chefs and their social connections. Yi once told me that the threshold to develop a Chinese restaurant was not high. As new restaurants were largely run by two or three chefs as co-owners, it was not difficult to achieve the entry threshold. However, most of them were lower-end restaurants. Strictly speaking, there was no up-market restaurant of all newly opened Chinese restaurants located within the university area. The only up-market restaurant in this area was founded in 2009 by a Hong Kong businessman, with elaborate decoration, cosy atmosphere, spacious room, comfortable sofas, etc. This restaurant was always full at dinner time due to its pleasant eating environment and limited choices from the market.

During my fieldwork in Firm D, Jack was planning to take over Firm D as the first step for his immigration. When it approached the end of my fieldwork, the procedure was already into the final stage. Jack had paid almost the full amount to Kate. Once he passed his visa application, he would become the owner. One day we discussed how to improve the business after his taking over. He told me:

> I already have some basic ideas. Once I take over, the first thing I will do is to refurbish it. All the current tables and chairs will be removed. Lights and ceiling will be entirely re-decorated. I will let customers clearly understand from the first impression that this is an up-market restaurant.
>
> Furthermore, I will change the menu as well. It will be no longer a fast food restaurant. I will retain the rice served with meat and vegetables because students have limited time during lunchtime. However, at dinner time, they prefer to eat some delicate food. They have money. They would like to eat in a relaxed environment with high-quality service. Is there any other restaurant like Firm D? It is absolutely ridiculous to order at the counter. I have got my plans in my mind.

As most of the Chinese restaurants provided similar food engaging in intense competition in the down-market, moving up-market would be one potential strategy. It has been identified that one of Firm U's advantages was its eating environment, although its location was a weakness, as it was far from the university area. A large number of Chinese students were from upper-middle-class families; they could afford a higher-end restaurant. However, the large amount of capital required to found an up-market restaurant made it impossible for chefs. By contrast, for those who had great wealth, such as Jack, investing an up-market restaurant in the university area would be a breakthrough in the competitive market.

Conclusions

This chapter examined how management in Sheffield's ethnic Chinese restaurant sector was affected by the product market. The sector developed quickly from 2011. On the demand side, there was a continuous growth of Chinese students. The student number in 2014 was five times more than it was in 2008. On the supply side, chefs seized the potential of the market and developed their own businesses.

The product market environment was unstable. Customer demands fluctuated following the pattern of university semesters. The demand was at a high level during semester time while at a low level during vacations. Labour management in small firms under an uncertain environment requires owners to make continuous adaptation (Edwards and Ram, 2006). In this turbulent environment, management strategies frequently adjusted to match the demand fluctuation. Two of the most influential practices were staff recruitment and dismissal. However, the actual adjustment process could not exactly fit the demand change model because labour costs were a big concern for owners. Their rationality for reducing costs resulted in two types of problems: employee dismissal before the transition from a high demand period to a low demand period and employee recruitment after the transition from a low demand period to a high demand period. The outcome was that the number of employees was always fewer than it should have been, which caused significant pressures upon workers and largely shaped management strategies in an imposed way.

The level of competition gradually became severe due to the sector's continuous expansion. Chinese restaurants rose from three to about 15 in less than four years in the university area. Excessive numbers of restaurants created market saturation. Strategic choices from owner-managers under the competitive environment were mainly examined from three aspects: pricing strategies, retaining customers and moving upward.

Because profit margins were limited by intense competition, one strategy to gain more profits was to raise prices after refurbishment, as both Firm D and Firm U had done. However, customers were sensitive to price change. The number of customers dropped significantly after prices went up. They soon set prices back and were forced to engage in price competition, which was largely the same as the South Asian restaurant sector (Jones et al., 2006). Enhancing service quality and retaining customers, therefore, became the minimum standard to gain some competitive advantages if there was not enough room to manoeuvre as far as the pricing strategy was concerned. However, because of its leading market position at early stages, Firm D failed to realise the importance of providing good service. It suffered a lot as a result.

Product markets serve to constrain, and meanwhile provide opportunities for management (Ram, 1994). Due to the reason that most Chinese restaurants competed in the down-market, moving upward was another opportunity for these Chinese restaurant owners. However, the high capital threshold was the main constraint for them to go to the up-end, especially for chefs. For those who held significant wealth, developing a higher-end Chinese restaurant in the university region could be a breakthrough for these entrepreneurs.

4 Influences From the Labour Market

Apart from the product market, the labour market also plays a crucial role in structuring management practices and employment relationships in small firms. Management control strategies were believed to be decided by the dependence of employers and employees, and workers' labour market power constituted an important element in the employment relationships (Goss, 1991b). Due to different levels of dependence, Moule (1998) identified that there was significant variation between despatch workers and dyers over the effort bargaining process. Additionally, the supply of particular workers, especially in ethnic firms, was critical in supporting business development and influencing their operating strategies. For example, large supplies of cheap female workers allowed businesses to compete in labour-intensive industries (Ram, 1994). The employment of illegal workers permitted ethnic firms to choose down market strategies (Ram et al., 2017b).

This chapter is to analyse how the labour market affected the day-to-day shop floor experiences and labour management strategies in the two restaurants. Section 1 examines the labour market context in the ethnic Chinese restaurant sector in Sheffield. The next three sections focus on three different groups of workers—chefs, kitchen assistants and front area workers—by discussing how the labour market shaped owner-managers' control strategies and to what extent labour could successfully negotiate for their interests. Conflict, consent and the dependence relationship between the two parties will be particularly analysed.

Labour Supply Shortage for Kitchen Staff and Its Implications

Chapter 3, when discussing the increase in the supply side, has identified that due to enough savings and entrepreneurial motivation, a large number of chefs started their own restaurants. This massively influenced the labour supply in the ethnic Chinese restaurant sector. The available chefs in the labour market were significantly reduced.

During the period of my fieldwork, Firm U's owner had been planning to introduce a general buffet (Firm U provided hot pot and skewer buffets, while the owner would like to also introduce a general buffet). Yi frequently discussed this with me. In the second week after Firm U re-opened after refurbishment, I asked Yi whether the buffet could be introduced soon. Yi answered:

> No way. There is no way to do a buffet next week. Now we (with another chef) need to cut and marinate all kinds of meat, which are used for skewers. If we are required to prepare a buffet, we cannot do skewers. There is too much work to do for the buffet. Two (chefs) is not enough at all. The minimum number for producing a buffet is three. He needs to at least recruit one more.

About one week later, Yi spoke to me:

> I'm dying. I've got a temperature. He (the owner) told me yesterday that he would like us to get the buffet done next week. He said he couldn't find any proper chef. He asked me to find one for him. Where am I supposed to find him a chef? If he cannot find a chef by next week and continues to ask me to do everything, I'm leaving.

In the third week, Yi talked about this again:

> Lewis, you know what? I previously worked in Newcastle on the buffet for five years. I knew everything about the buffet. If he believes two is okay, we can have a try. However, he still asked me to prepare skewer meat, telling me that he couldn't find a decent chef. Anyway, if he finally decides to do a buffet, I will only do the buffet. If the meat for skewers cannot be prepared on time, that is none of my business. I do not have a responsibility to find a chef for him. I already got Dong (the other chef, Yi's friend) here. I've got a UK passport. If he keeps pressuring me, I will leave. I can find a job with ease.

The owner finally failed to find a proper chef until the end of my fieldwork. There had been no buffet in Firm U by the time I finished my research there.

As mentioned in Chapter 2, Firm D's owners were a couple. Kate worked in the front area, while her husband Nick worked in the kitchen as the head chef. Kate indeed often interfered in kitchen management. For example, if she found the amount of a dish was too much or if she thought a dish was not tidy before delivering, she would go into the kitchen and shout at kitchen staff. One day, probably because she felt that the cooking speed was too slow, she suddenly walked into the kitchen from the counter and shouted: 'Be quick! Be quick!' Nick followed her out and angrily spoke to her:

> Shut up! If you continue acting like this and lead to their departure, where do you find replacements? I'm in charge of the kitchen. You'd better only focus on the front area. Don't mess up the kitchen!

Nick obviously worried that the business would struggle if the existing kitchen staff left because of Kate's bad manner in management. Under the situation of labour supply shortage, the departure of kitchen staff might cause huge uncertainties to these Chinese restaurants. Take my experience for example—the owner was keen to recruit me because two chefs were planning to leave when I negotiated for the access. He could not find any kitchen worker from the labour market. I was the only choice although I knew nothing about kitchen work. A short supply of kitchen workers in the sector was confirmed by Yi:

> Generally speaking, it is. However, there is a difference between kitchen assistants and chefs. For kitchen assistants, it is not very difficult. Look, you can even be a proper assistant. Even for chefs, I would say finding a chef is not as difficult as you imagine. However, the most important problem is that it is really hard to find a good chef.
>
> See Juan (Juan worked in Firm U for two weeks as a head chef before flying back to China). Because the owner at that time couldn't find a chef, he recruited him from the web. Juan said he had previously worked in London's China Town. Are you kidding me? If he says this to you, to customers, well, that is okay. I have been a chef for nearly 20 years. He is absolutely shit. See the fucking noodles he cooked. It is impossible for a decent chef to cook like that. No flavour at all. He was also lazy. You know this, right? Watching movies for the entire day using his tablet. You know what? I would like to let him go in the first week. However, the owner couldn't find any proper chef, so he stayed for another week.

So far, the discussion has demonstrated that inadequate supplies of kitchen workers created a series of problems for ethnic Chinese restaurants. According to Yi, finding a chef, especially a skilled chef, was really difficult. Having understood the environment, the next sections will discuss how the labour market influenced negotiation power and the effort bargaining process between owner-managers and workers.

Kitchen Assistants' Labour Market Positions and Their Negotiation Power

The analysis starts by reviewing two cases I have mentioned in Chapter 3.

The first case: Gui was a part-time kitchen assistant in Firm D. She was dismissed before Christmas by the 'early adjustment' principle as the business was to experience a low demand period at Christmas.

The second case: When Firm U re-opened after refurbishment in late May, there were three kitchen workers. The owner soon recruited one kitchen assistant because it was during the high customer demand period. It soon went into June, when the demand began to drop. The owner came to the site in mid-June and sacked the kitchen assistant.

Both of the cases largely described the vulnerable labour market positions of kitchen assistants. In the face of the demand fluctuation, they were easily sacked. Even if the labour market was short of supply, they had little power in negotiating for their job security. The decision-making for sacking a kitchen assistant was dominated by owners. Apart from job security, kitchen assistants also had limited scope for wage bargaining.

This chapter in the beginning has mentioned that I secured my access to Firm U because two kitchen workers were about to leave. They were a couple; the male was a chef, and the female was an assistant. I had asked them why they would like to depart. They did not elaborate on the reasons, just saying that they had a conflict with the owner. Yi later told me that it was because of the wage issue. The couple felt that due to the reduction of kitchen staff, they had to complete lots of extra work such as washing pots. They thought they should receive more pay as a result. The weekly wage of the female assistant had been £300. She applied for a wage increase to £350 a week; the owner rejected the request. She then tried £330; the owner did not agree to that either. The owner refused to raise the kitchen assistant's wage at the risk of losing two out of three kitchen staff, and meanwhile there was no available replacement at that moment.

Two weeks before I finished my fieldwork in Firm U, Yi began to search for a replacement to take over my job. I asked Yi whether £300 per week was a bit low to find any decent kitchen assistants, Yi replied:

> If it was a few years ago, I would say yes. For one holding a UK passport, the minimum would be £340. However, things have changed. There was a country. Erm, I cannot remember its name. It collapsed around two years ago. The UK government accepted most of its residents. Some of them are now working in Chinese restaurants. See the guy working in firm T (Yi previously worked there). He was from that country. He was paid £200 per week. He needs to work over ten hours a day, washing dishes, cutting meat and vegetables and cleaning everything. He has been working there over a year. He is happy for £200 a week. Many

have asked me about your job. Although most of them in the beginning expressed that it was a little bit low, they finally would like to take the job. They knew that if they did not choose the job, somebody would do. They were aware that the wage for kitchen assistants was at this level.

All kitchen assistants in Firm U were paid £300 a week, regardless of their work intensity. The wage standard, according to Yi, was set by the labour market. Labour supplies for ethnic Chinese restaurants in recent years were filled with other ethnic minorities. Ethnic Chinese labour had to compete with them to get a job. However, workers from other ethnic groups were happy to accept a wage far lower than the amount given to ethnic Chinese labour. This further weakened their negotiation power over wage bargaining. Discussions in this section seem to demonstrate that there was no room for workers to negotiate for a pay rise, even in extreme conditions. The following evidence supported the analysis.

Teng and his wife started to work in Firm U a week after I had arrived. His wife was a pot washer; he was a kitchen assistant. It was extremely busy on an evening shift. Having finished all the tasks, Teng looked exhausted. I joked with him:

> Go and see the owner. Ask him to increase your wage.

Teng answered:

> Yes, it is necessary to speak to the owner about this. Look, he (Juan, the chef who was believed to be lazy, working in Firm U for two weeks before going back to China) earns £450; I get £300. I work far more than he does. I've got to ask the owner what's wrong with the kitchen.

On the next day, Teng was asked to do a fruit mix for karaoke customers at about 9 PM, when he had just finished nearly four hours of cooking. He spoke to me:

> I need to do everything. The one who earns £450 does nothing. I earn £300, doing everything. I will phone the owner to discuss this with him. I am planning to negotiate with him for my wage increase.

When the owner came to collect money on the second week, he had a talk with Teng after work. I texted Teng that evening and asked him whether his negotiation was successful. Teng phoned me back, saying:

> Yes, he agreed to increase my wage to £350, but it is not a 'free' rise. Juan will leave next week. After that, Yi will become the head chef. I will take over the job Yi is currently doing, as an assistant chef.

However, Yi was paid £450 a week. Wage bargaining for Teng appeared to get him more pay; it indeed strengthened the system of managerial control. It reinforced the management structure over kitchen assistants. Structural conditions largely limited kitchen assistants' wage bargaining due to their subordinate labour market position. The owner kept the bargaining process strictly within his control.

A week later, the owner decided to refurbish the restaurant. Two weeks through the re-decoration, I received a text from Teng, saying: 'I am leaving tomorrow'. I called him out and had dinner with him. Teng said:

> I cannot continue waiting. I need to get a new job to earn money. Nobody knows when it re-opens. I met him this morning. I said I was planning to leave as I cannot keep waiting. He said nothing, but okay. There was no 'Thanks'; there was no word trying to keep me. I told him I would like to leave my wife here. He refused.
>
> I have been so committed to him, to the business since I came. But, maybe he thinks that is what I should do. I can still remember how he persuaded me to work here. I definitely had value for him at that time; he could not find other workers. Now, he must believe he has enough time to find any replacement before the decoration is ready. Otherwise, he wouldn't let me go.

About a month after Teng had left Firm U, I had a conversation with the owner aiming to understand his attitudes about his decision. He told me:

> He only worked in the UK for less than half a year. He did not understand the culture at all. He did not understand what wage level he belonged to. I'm telling you, I was already very kind to him, but he was still unsatisfied. If he believed that he should get more, it's better for him to go and see what the sector is like.

Teng's departure confirmed the point that there was domination of labour management over kitchen assistants. Teng's suggestion that he would leave was regarded as resistance by the owner. Wage-effort bargaining from Teng was not acceptable to the owner under the managerial structure.

Although the labour shortage was the problem for most ethnic Chinese restaurants, there had been a low level of dependence of owners upon kitchen assistants. Kitchen assistants were in a weak labour market position, which determined the power imbalance between them and owner-managers. Their subordinate position largely constrained their negotiation power. Structural limits from the labour market meant that employee resistance was difficult.

Negotiation over wage bargaining was not acceptable to owners. The fact that dismissal and replacement could be easily conducted gave employees little choice but to be compliant. Decision-making was dominated by owners.

Chefs' Labour Market Positions and Their Negotiation Power

Yi once described the ethnic Chinese restaurant sector in one sentence:

> In the UK, it is the chefs that choose owners.

According to Yi's statement, chefs seemed to have the dominant labour market position and were expected to have strong bargaining power. Empirical data from this study largely proved this.

The last section mentioned that Teng failed to save his job in Firm U during the re-decoration period. Let's now examine Yi's experience during the same period. Yi stayed in Firm U after the re-decoration. After the business re-opened, I asked Yi why he chose to stay. Yi answered:

> He (the owner) frequently phoned me. I told him that I would like to leave. I have a family. I need to earn money. I told him I just couldn't wait. It is annoying. I said I could not keep waiting. I've got to support my family and pay my loan. He later told me that he would like to offer me £200 a week during the decoration period and promised to increase my weekly wage from £450 to £480 afterwards.

'Then, it looks like he is highly dependent upon you', I said. Yi replied:

> He is not exactly reliant on me. Every chef knows how to do the work. The problem is that he cannot find any proper chef. I bring Dong here (Dong was the chef Yi found during the decoration period). He has nowhere to find any good chefs. Moreover, you know what? Dong lives in Derby. He (the owner) needs to pay for his accommodation in Sheffield. It's about £200 a month. That means he needs to spend extra £50 a week for him. I live here (Sheffield). That wouldn't cost him anymore.
>
> Every owner here is the same. Purely capitalist. You know what? When I worked in Firm T previously, my initial wage was £410. I said I would like to leave; the owner added £20 on my wage. Next time, I said I would like to leave, he added £20 again. For the third time, I said I would like to leave. He said: Yi, don't leave; don't leave. He added another £30. When I finally left Firm T, my weekly wage was £480. I

am telling you, they are all shit. If you do not put pressure on them, they will never increase your wage.

In June 2015, Dong left Firm U after finding a job in Derby. Yi became the only chef. The owner later raised his wage. I asked him whether he actively negotiated for a pay rise. Yi replied to me:

> It's surely I bargained with him. Dong has already left. I need to do everything. I am definitely worth to get more. There is no way I get the same. He's got to pay me more. Otherwise, do you expect I will stay?

When Teng expressed that he would like to leave during the refurbishment period, the owner did not retain him at all. However, there was a significant difference when Yi expressed the same idea. The owner not only increased his wage but also compensated him for temporary rest during the decoration period, which was £200 per week, nearly half of his weekly income. Yi's claim of departure was indeed a way of negotiation. If he had decided to leave, he would have left without hesitation. He knew that the owner would not let him go. The threat of departure successfully helped him to achieve wage bargaining. After Dong had left, Yi negotiated with the owner over a pay rise for the second time. Due to being highly dependent upon him, the owner compromised with Yi on the wage issue and was forced to raise his wage again.

In Firm D, direct effort bargaining and workplace resistance form chefs were dramatic. As mentioned in Chapter 3, Jack was planning to take over the business during my fieldwork. One day when we were chatting, he said to me:

> You know what? Kang (a female chef in Firm D) has begun to directly challenge Kate. It's been hot recently. If there was no order, they (chefs) normally sit outside, instead of staying in the kitchen. Yesterday, when they were chatting, Kate gave them two orders. Lu (another chef) went back to the kitchen immediately to start cooking. Kate told Kang that there was another order. Kang said to Kate that Lu was enough to cook two dishes. She then kept sitting on the chair, entirely ignoring Kate's instruction.
>
> She knows the business will be sold out soon, so she doesn't care. You know what? I would like to sack Huo (a kitchen assistant) after I take over. However, Huo is very close to Kang. Once Huo is gone, my concern is that Kang might leave as well.

'Is that a big deal if Kang leaves?' I asked him. Jack hesitated for a second, speaking to me:

Yes, she is in charge of the stocking. She is now fully managing the kitchen. I need to keep her for a while at least. Finding a decent chef was not easy.

Sacking a kitchen assistant might be straightforward. However, if a kitchen assistant had a tight relationship with a chef, there might be consequences. The evidence above illustrated the extent to which chefs' labour market position could exert influences on owner-managers choices.

During the final stage of my fieldwork in Firm D, my shifts reduced. I heard a lot of stories from Jack:

> Yesterday, Kate irritated kitchen staff again. The thing is that it was not busy on the lunch shift. She used his phone to check the CCTV, which showed the record the day before. When Gui (a kitchen assistant) went out to pick up water from the counter, she moved the phone away from his ear in order to prevent Gui from noticing this. However, it turned into the speaker mode. Gui heard that and told this to kitchen staff.

I asked Jack whether this meant that Kate did not trust them. Jack answered:

> Yes. Last time when they (kitchen staff) stocked, they secretly put some meat into their bags and took it away after work. Kate saw everything from the CCTV. She said to me in anger. Additionally, whenever they steamed pork ribs, they would take some away. Kate knew this, as well. However, she never exposes these tricks. She is afraid of losing them.

In this context where there had been a short supply of available labour, resistance and effort bargaining from kitchen assistants were hardly accepted by owners. By contrast, power dynamics between owners and chefs were significantly different. Due to owners' high degrees of dependence on them, chefs actively engaged with direct wages-effort bargaining. Chefs' dominant labour market position gave them strong power to negotiate for their interests. Owners' authority was challenged on a variety of occasions. The labour market also significantly influenced the owner's attitudes and control strategies for chefs. Owners were unwilling to have conflicts with chefs. Firm D's owner even had to tolerate the chefs' fiddles. She would rather pretend not to know of their fiddles, instead of revealing their cheatings and sacking them. They knew finding a skilled chef was tough in the sector. Yi's word at the beginning of this section did not exaggerate the chefs' negotiation power.

Front Area Staff's Labour Market Position and Their Negotiation Power

Power Dynamics

A week after I started my fieldwork in Firm U, Yi and I had a chat about my working experiences in Firm D. I discussed with him several of Firm D's management practices:

> Sometimes when a part-time worker started his shift at 6 PM, the owner might let him go at 8 PM if there were few customers (the evening shift was from 6 PM to 10 PM). They could earn a little by working just for two hours.

Yi said:

> That's normal. Every restaurant is the same in Sheffield. There are so many students on the waiting list. If any of them does not want to do the job, no owner cares. Too many want to get a part-time job. By contrast, full-time workers have lots more value. It's not very easy to find a good full-time worker.

During my fieldwork in Firm D and Firm U, I altogether had worked with over 15 part-time front area workers. Students constituted 100% of the employment. By contrast, the employment of full-time workers was stable. Jack had been the only full-time front area worker in Firm D. Firm U had employed two full-time workers, one before the refurbishment and one after. Yi's words identified a difference between full-time workers and part-time student workers in their values. Empirical data suggested part-time student employees were easy to replace, and their negotiation power was extremely weak, while full-time workers had strong power to engage in wage-bargaining.

After working in Firm D for a week, I found that Jack sometimes would put a few coins into a small bucket at the counter, rather than put them in the till. I asked him what the bucket was used for. He told me that it was the tips bucket. When a customer left a tip, the tips were shared by full-time front area workers and the owner. After his explanation, Jack told me some more stories:

> There was no 'tips sharing' policy at the beginning. Tips originally completely belonged to Kate. Erm, do you remember that girl, who was short, wearing a pair of glasses? She worked here a year ago as a full-time waiter. Can you remember her? (I said yes, and I described the girl

a little bit.) Spot on! It was her. Her name is Sonia. She is Malaysian. She could speak Mandarin, Cantonese and English fluently, and she was experienced. After working here for a while, she one day asked for a pay rise. However, Kate wouldn't want to increase her wage. I cannot remember what exactly happened then, you know. It seemed that they had an argument about this. Finally, they reached the agreement that Sonia's wage would keep the same, while tips would be shared among full-time workers, including me. It was no longer Kate's revenue. The bucket has been here since then.

According to Jack, after Sonia's departure, Kate tried another full-time worker. However, Kate was dissatisfied with her performance after using her for a while and later sacked the girl. Since then, she had not found a full-time worker. With a short supply of full-time workers, they could exert strong impacts on the wage-bargaining process. Negotiation power for part-time workers was, however, considerably limited.

Han had five shifts in the first week of working in Firm D as a part-time front area worker. However, both Kate and Jack were not satisfied with her performance. About a week later, two former part-time workers returned. Jack decided to reduce Han's shifts. In the second week, Han's shifts were down to two. Unfortunately, Han did not improve her ability. As a result, Jack planned to sack her. He said to me:

> I will not put her on the roster next week. I will not send her a notice message.

Han worked only once in the third week due to Kate's day off. Jack never called her back from the fourth week.

Shang was one of the two returned part-time employees. Because Shang had worked in Firm D for one semester, she knew the service procedures. She quickly became a regular part-time employee. After Han had been dropped from the roster, Shang took over Han's shifts. Shang told Kate that she could do lunch shifts in the fourth week from Monday to Friday. Kate agreed. However, Shang did not appear on the Monday's lunch shift in the following week. Kate tried to contact her several times, but she did not get through. Shang called back later in the day saying that she had not received a message from Jack about the arrangement of her shifts. This made both Kate and Jack very angry as Shang had agreed to work on lunch shifts from Monday to Friday starting from the fourth week. Due to this incident, Jack made the decision to reduce Shang's shifts.

Fei joined Firm D in the third week. He was a second choice on the roster in the beginning. After Shang's case, Kate asked Fei whether he could regularly work on lunch shifts. Fei told Kate he could do it from Monday to Thursday. Because Shang had already lost Kate's favour, Fei became a regular part-time employee as replacement of Shang.

However, as he worked more shifts, more problems emerged. His working pace was below average. Moreover, Kate was a Cantonese speaker, while Fei was a Mandarin speaker. As a result, Fei could hardly understand Kate's words (further discussion about the language problem is in Chapter 5). Kate gradually became impatient with him. She finally could not bear him because he frequently committed mistakes. Since Jack later had introduced his friend to work in Firm D, Fei was back to a second choice.

The experiences of Han, Shang and Fei were similar. Although all of them had quite a few shifts in the beginning, none of them sustained for a long time. Each was easily replaced. As long as the owner lost her patience, the strategy was to reduce their shifts and get someone else to take over. Once Kate and Jack had made the decision, there was no scope for them to negotiate. They had no choices but to consent.

After Firm U's re-decoration, Zha, the front area manager, suggested the owner get back former experienced employees. The owner, however, rejected his suggestion. He decided to recruit new part-time workers, instead of continuing to employ any of the former staff. Within two days after putting a recruitment note on the window, six students went to ask for a part-time job. Finding a part-time student worker was rather easy.

Yu was one of the students selected by Zha. Before working in Firm U, he had worked in several different Chinese restaurants. He believed owners' strategies towards managing part-time workers were the same everywhere:

> I took a part-time job in Firm L prior to coming here. Because my girlfriend had been working there, I knew the owner. He invited me to work for him. In my first week, I was given five shifts. Due to unfamiliarity with the servicing procedure, I committed a mistake. The owner was beside me. It was not fucking serious at all! When the roster for the second week was released, there was no shift for me. The manager told me the owner asked him to remove all my shifts.

Yu had exactly the same experience as a part-time worker in Firm D. As there had been large numbers of students who were willing to take a part-time job in the ethnic Chinese restaurant sector, owners did not worried about recruiting front area part-time workers. Moreover, being a waiter did not require substantial skills. Owners, as a result, had little dependence upon them. Dismissing a part-time student employee could happen at any time for any reason by the owner. Students in the face of owners' imposed control could hardly engage in any negotiation for their interests. Employment relations between part-time workers and owner-managers were dominated by owners' opinions based on the nature of the labour market.

The Significance of Employing Students for Owners

During my entire working period in the two firms, the National Minimum Wage was £6.50 per hour for those over 21 and £5.13 per hour for those between 18 and 21 (National Minimum Wage, 2015). However, in both Firm D and Firm U, the wage for part-time student employees was £5 an hour. All part-time workers received a wage less than the NMW. Indeed, Firm D's initial weekly wage started from £4.50. If the owner believed a worker turned skilled, she would increase it to £5. The last section has demonstrated that there had been a pool of candidates waiting on the list. With a large number of students willing to work for low pay, student workers were important for ethnic Chinese restaurant owners to significantly reduce labour costs.

Furthermore, part-time student workers in ethnic Chinese restaurants enabled owners to conduct flexible control. In Firm D, the lunch shift was set from 12 PM to 3 PM, and the dinner shift was from 6 PM to 10 PM. As Firm D's main customer base was lunchtime customers, part-time workers could normally work the entire lunch shift. However, working hours on the dinner shift were always flexible according to the number of customers. For most of the time during my fieldwork in Firm D, part-time front area employees were asked to leave at 9 PM. The owner would sometimes let them go at 8 PM, after working only two hours. A few students expressed dissatisfaction with this type of flexible management as they earned less. However, their subordinate labour market position decided that they had to accept 'flexibility' if they would like to continue their work.

My job in Firm D was somewhere between a full-time worker and a part-time worker. I generally did my lunch shift from 11 AM to 3 PM and started my dinner shift at 5 PM, working longer hours than a part-time worker and not working as a full-time worker because I had a two-hour break between 3 PM and 5 PM. Jack commented on my work type:

> You are indeed a part-time worker. Your wage is calculated by hours, right? She (the owner) wouldn't want to pay you for those two hours because it was not busy during that period. If you work as a full-time worker (weekly wage, not hourly wage), there is no way that she would let you go. It is impossible. You may even work up to 11 hours a day.

Because Firm U's owner was always absent, the front area was managed by Zha. However, Zha also had his own business. This meant that although he was allowed to have one day off a week, he was generally away at least two days a week. In these days, he used part-time workers to cover his job. Zha expressed his opinions when we discussed a girl:

> Yes, you are right. I don't like her. The reason why I asked her to come today is that I went to do my business this morning. I need to find a part-time worker to cover my job. Otherwise, it is impossible for me to call her. She only has this much value. That's why I didn't remove her from the list.

By employing part-time student employees, Chinese restaurants could effectively adapt to the unstable market. Owners could carry out flexible control over working hours, which facilitated significant costs reduction. It would have been impossible if full-time workers were widely used. Additionally, using part-time workers had various meanings of everyday practices. It could ease the management based on a firm's specific context.

Ethnic Chinese Restaurants as the Opportunity for Students

Throughout my entire fieldwork, I had a detailed discussion with a total of nine students in the two sites. I aimed to understand what drove them to become part-time front area workers. Although some in the beginning were reluctant to acknowledge that their primary aim was to earn money, by asking them a few further questions, all of them finally expressed that the fundamental reason to take a part-time job was to get some extra money:

> It's not just £5 an hour. They provide me with meals after I finish my shifts. If I work two shifts at weekends, I don't need to spend on buying food. This saves a lot. You buy takeaways every day, right? You know the price. If you buy meals which are as good as the food we eat here, it would at least cost you £10.
>
> (one student)

> Indeed, I did not have any plan to work as a part-time employee at the beginning. However, I would like to buy an iPhone 6 for my boyfriend as his birthday gift. I didn't have that much money at that time. I didn't want to ask for the money from my parents, either. They already spent a lot on supporting my study. That is why I started to become a part-time worker for the first time two years ago.
>
> (another student)

One mentioned that she only worked one shift a week. I wondered whether £20 per week was too little. She replied:

I'm happy with £20 a week. That's okay. It's nearly £100 a month. That's quite a lot indeed.

After working as a part-time worker, three out of nine stopped economic support from their families. These three students were all in their dissertation stage, so they could fully control their time. They worked at least four days a week; one worked up to five days. Their weekly wage was around £200. The highest could earn as much as £250 a week. One of them told me:

My dissertation is approaching the end. By working here, I don't need to ask for money from my parents. I'm from an ordinary family. I feel guilty to keep asking for money from them. I'm already 24. My weekly wage can cover the rent and my basic needs.

Of all the nine students, two had previously applied for a part-time job in a non-Chinese enterprise. One told me:

I previously had an interview for a cafe job. Having finished the interview, the manager told me that there was a girl from Mexico applying for the job and she can speak fluent English. After listening to this, I knew I lost the chance.

The other said:

I sent my CV to several pubs. They asked me to wait to be contacted. None of them contacted me at the end. Well, that's fair enough. Why would they employ me if there are so many British willing to work for them?

Except for these two, no one had ever made an application for non-Chinese businesses. A detailed interview with each of them revealed that they generally did not think of being a part-time worker in a non-Chinese restaurant. They said:

I just never thought to be an employee in British firms. Just never have the thought.
Erm, I don't know. It is easy to find a job in Chinese restaurants.
I'm scared of working with whites. Maybe this is the reason.
Probably I think I'm not competent. Well, I dunno.

Apart from the different reasons above, there was also one common answer: 'I think my English level is not qualified enough to get a job in British firms'. Chinese students understood that their language skill was a critical reason preventing them from being employed in non-Chinese businesses. Their English skills largely constrained alternative choices. Against this background, Chinese restaurants provided students with the opportunity to get a paid job, although the wage was less than the NMW standard. It was essential to reduce economic pressures for those from an ordinary family. With the significant increase in ethnic Chinese restaurants, more Chinese students had the chance to take a part-time job to support their living.

Conclusions

This chapter examined how the labour market shaped the management practices and employment relations in the ethnic Chinese restaurant sector. Chapter 3 mentioned that there had been a continuous rise of ethnic Chinese restaurants in Sheffield. Owners of these new restaurants were mostly chefs. Due to their departure, existing Chinese restaurants faced serious problems in recruiting kitchen workers. As a result, there had been a short supply of kitchen workers in the sector.

In the ethnic Chinese restaurant sector, owners had low levels of reliance upon kitchen assistants, regardless of the labour shortage. Kitchen assistants were in a vulnerable labour market position. Their subordinate position largely constrained their negotiation power. Owners had substantial authority over them. Decisions such as dismissal and replacement were regularly conducted in the face of the demand fluctuation. Negotiation over wage bargaining was not acceptable by owners. None of the kitchen assistants successfully negotiated for a pay rise during the period of the field work.

By contrast, ethnic Chinese restaurant owners had high levels of dependence upon chefs. They had much greater job security than kitchen assistants. Their superior labour market position enabled them to actively engage in negotiation over rewards and wages. Management practices were largely shaped according to chefs' desires. Explicit resistances in both restaurants were carried out in various ways. Firm D's owner could even tolerate fiddles by not having direct conflicts with chefs in fear of their departure. Jack had concerns over sacking a kitchen assistant as this might make him lose a chef due to their close relationship. Because of the short supply from the labour market and owners' high levels of dependence, chefs had strong negotiation powers in wage-effort bargaining.

Part-time front area workers in these two sites were completely comprised of students. Due to the large supply of students, owners had little dependence on them. Kitchen assistants at least might secure their jobs during a high demand period, while student workers could be replaced at any time. Managerial control under this situation was simply imposed. In the face of the structural constraint, they had little power to positively respond to autocratic management.

Goss (1991a) suggested that management strategies in regulating labour are strongly affected by the level of dependence. By analysing their different labour market positions and different levels of owners' dependence, this chapter demonstrated how consent and conflict developed on the shop floor for three different groups of workers.

Additionally, this chapter also examined the significance of employing students as front area workers for ethnic Chinese restaurants. First, labour costs for part-time workers were much lower than employing full-time workers. Second, part-time workers enabled owner-managers to conduct flexible control. Owners could adjust the number of workers hourly according to the number of customers each day. It gave owners the chance to quickly adapt to environmental change to run their businesses effectively. With these two reasons, part-time student employees functioned to massively reduce labour costs in the ethnic Chinese restaurant sector.

The value of Chinese restaurants to students was also great. The primary reason for students to search for a job was to alleviate economic pressures on their families. Due to their language constraint, students had limited choices in the market. The expansion of Chinese restaurants provided significant employment opportunities for them. Taking a part-time job in Chinese restaurants covered their living expenses to a large extent.

5 Multi-Cultural Workforces

The Chinese community in Britain is composed of groups with diverse origins and cultural backgrounds. There are three main groups: people from Hong Kong and Guangdong province (a province in Southern China) who mainly speak Cantonese; people from China's other provinces who speak Mandarin; and British-born Chinese (BBC), for whom English is their first language. It was suggested that there were potentially tensions between different group members (Chan et al., 2007).

This chapter examines how the racial context shaped their workplace behaviours and employment relationships in the two restaurants. The chapter is structured into three sections. Section 1 describes the communication problems among different groups of people and analyses how the language barrier created difficulties in workplace control. Guessing and intersubjectivity played a central role in accommodating workers to owners' perceptions. Section 2 analyses the variation of owners' trust towards members from different groups and the implications to control strategies. The final section focuses on the inter-group conflicts. It discusses how conflicts and tensions caused by the cultural difference were experienced vertically between owners and workers and horizontally between workers and workers.

Communication Problems

Different Languages Being Used

Based on evidence from this research, Table 5.1 shows the ability of each group of people in the two restaurants to understand and speak different dialects.

According to the table, understanding and speaking Mandarin and English were generally not a problem for all the three groups of people. By contrast, Cantonese would create difficulties in communication. For ordinary

Table 5.1 The Ability of Understanding and Speaking Different Languages

	Mandarin	*Cantonese*	*English*
Mandarin speakers	Great	Poor	Moderate
Cantonese speakers	Moderate	Great	Moderate
British-born Chinese	Moderate	Depends on the parents' background	Great

Mandarin speakers, they could hardly understand and speak Cantonese. For British-born Chinese, their parents' background decided whether they had ability in understanding and speaking Cantonese. If one of their parents had the Cantonese background, they had no difficulty in understanding and speaking Cantonese. If none of their parents had a Cantonese background, it was unlikely that a British-born Chinese person would have the ability to understand and speak Cantonese.

Firm U's owner was a Mandarin speaker from Tianjin municipality, a northern city of China. He moved to the UK about ten years ago. Due to his social experiences after he had arrived in the UK, he later learned how to speak Cantonese. When he appeared at the restaurant, he spoke Cantonese when communicating with Cantonese speaking workers and used Mandarin when talking to Mandarin speakers. Chefs in Firm U were from Guangdong province, with a Cantonese background. All of them could speak Mandarin fluently as well. When they talked to each other, they spoke Cantonese; when they talked to Mandarin speakers, they switched to Mandarin. Dialect differences in Firm U were, therefore, not a barrier in communication.

Communication in Firm D was, however, a major problem. Both Kate and Nick, Firm D's couple owners, were from Hong Kong. They spoke Cantonese and could hardly speak Mandarin. Jack, the front area manager in Firm D, was a Mandarin speaker from Xi'an, a north-western Chinese city. Due to his Mandarin background, he could not understand and speak Cantonese in the beginning. Having worked in Firm D for years with every-day contact with Kate and Nick, Jack gained the ability to understand basic Cantonese, although he could speak only a little. As a result, communication between him and Kate was fine. I am a Mandarin speaker. Like most Mandarin speakers in this study, I was not capable of understanding and speaking Cantonese. When I initially started my fieldwork in Firm D, the owner always spoke Cantonese to me. Having realised I could not understand, she began to speak English. So, the communication between Kate and me was always starting from Cantonese, soon switching to English. This type of communication had lasted quite a long time until I could gradually understand some of her words based on routine work. Even in this condition, English was still the necessary tool to connect us. The communication between Kate and other Mandarin speakers also highly relied on English.

Although English could facilitate communication to some extent, it did not fundamentally solve the problem. During my fieldwork, two BBCs had worked in Firm D as part-time front area workers. Zoe was one of them. With her parents both of Mandarin background, she could not speak Cantonese. Communication between Kate and Zoe was always conducted in English. However, as Zoe was a native speaker, Kate sometimes could not understand Zoe's words. The communication between them was therefore complex. Jack always worked as an interpreter as a result. When Kate spoke Cantonese to Zoe, Jack translated Cantonese into Mandarin to Zoe.

Due to the language barrier, Kate had serious communication problems with non-Cantonese speakers. 'Guessing' played a crucial role for employees to understand Kate's instructions. The mutual adjustment was considerably affected by the process of guessing.

From Guessing to Adaptation

A week before I finished my fieldwork in Firm D, I had a discussion with Fei, a Mandarin front area worker in Firm D. I asked him whether his Cantonese had improved. He said:

> Of course not. I can guess 50% of her words. For the remaining 50%, I just literally cannot understand at all.

A similar idea was expressed by another Mandarin speaking worker, Cui. I one day chatted with her about whether she was frightened of Kate because Kate's attitude towards her was not always friendly. She said:

> No, I'm not bothered at all because I do not understand any of her words. When she speaks to me, I just nod and say okay. I just read her facial expression and keep smiling. That's it.

In a situation where Cantonese could not be easily understood by Mandarin speaking workers, it was normal for workers to draw on the perception of the owner's value or interests to respond. During this process, the unspoken influences and guessing largely influenced their behaviours in adaptation. Both Fei and Cui tried to understand Kate's words by guessing what she was saying in a particular context. The concept of intersubjectivity was extremely important to understand how people from different backgrounds accommodated each other.

One day when the lunch shift had finished, I stood near the counter reading news from my mobile phone. Kate suddenly called my name and spoke to me. As mentioned above, I did not understand her words during the early stage of my fieldwork. I noticed that she was carrying a bottle of detergent and a few tissues in her hands. However, this just simply could not give me a clue to what she would like me to do. After a few words, she seemed to realise that I did not understand. Her face turned suddenly to an expression of obvious impatience. She walked directly to a round table and began to wipe the glass on that table. I then understood her meaning. I followed her to the table and took the tissues and detergent from her, starting to clean. It could be read from her face that she felt upset. After handing the cleaning stuff to me, she did not even have a look at me and walked back.

The same thing happened for the second time about one week later. It was also at the end of a lunch shift. Kate held the detergent and tissues speaking to me again. Although I still could not understand her words, I knew her meaning this time. I got the cleaning stuff from her and went to clean the glass. She said nothing, which meant that it was exactly what she would like me to do.

Firm D provided hot pot as well, although it was not its main business. Due to the speciality of the hot pot, the normal chopsticks needed to be changed into special ones for hot pot use. Moreover, one extra small bowl and a large plate had to be provided. As mentioned in Chapter 3, Firm D carried out on-the-job training. The owner would teach a worker step-by-step the hot pot serving procedure when the worker served the hot pot for the first time. After that, workers were asked to serve customers by themselves. However, the steps were not easy to remember after being taught only once. When Han served hot pot customers by herself for the first time, she forgot two things: changing chopsticks and providing a large plate. After Han had been back to the counter, Kate began to speak to her in Cantonese. Han, as the Mandarin speaker, could not understand Kate's words. She just looked at Kate with a blank expression on her face. Kate soon realised that Han did to understand her meanings. She rushed out from the counter and began to serve the hot pot customers by herself. Having seen this, Han said sorry to Kate and promised Kate she had remembered the steps.

When Han served hot pot for the second time, she forgot to give customers the hot pot menu, although she completed all other procedures correctly. This irritated Kate again. She shouted at Han at the counter and kept telling her that it was the wrong menu. Having experienced the similar incident previously, Han immediately went back to double-check the table setting. Because the problem was not caused by table setting, having finished the checking, Han told Kate that she thought everything was okay. Kate looked extremely unhappy. She switched to English, saying 'menu, menu'. Han suddenly realised her mistake and kept apologising to Kate.

When it was towards the end of my fieldwork in Firm D, I could understand a few Cantonese words. One day when Fei was transferring bottled drinks from original packages into the fridge, due to his carelessness, he overturned the box and bottles were everywhere on the floor. Kate was standing inside the counter when this happened. Having seen this, she asked Fei to be careful. In addition, she found that Fei had put some drinks into the wrong places in the fridge. She then spent some time telling Fei the right places for each type of drinks. Fei kept nodding and said okay when listening to Kate's instructions. Just after Kate had been back to the counter, Fei overturned the box again. Kate this time turned furious. She shouted at Fei and kept asking him why he messed up everything. Nervousness and anxiety could be read from Fei's face. He just repeated sorry and meanwhile cleaned the mess.

When the shift approached the end, I went to get Fei and asked him why he frequently made mistakes. Fei said with a deep sigh:

> I admitted that I made a mistake in the beginning. However, did you see how she spoke to me after that? She just kept blaming me, standing there shouting at me. That made me so scared. If she had not done that, I would have been all right.

I told him:

> No, she just said that you should put everything in the right places. She asked you to be careful. She didn't take your mistake so seriously.

Fei hesitated for a second and said:

> I did not know. I did not understand her words. You know she has been harsh. I just thought she was blaming me. This gave me huge pressure and made me so nervous. That's why I messed it up again. It's so annoying.

Ambiguities arising from employees' failure to understand Cantonese limited the extent to which Kate could directly control the serving process. Workers' responses to Kate's commands were largely based on guesses. Employees had to make assumptions about the owner's perceptions and intentions. The adaptation that took place from the employees to Kate was informed by the ongoing subjective guessing rather than by explicit oral communication. In the absence of explicit communication, a variety of actions relied heavily on subjective interpretation and recognition. The owners' interests and objectives were often assumed by employees based on their previous working experiences. This formed an important part of the ongoing, everyday behaviours. However, adaptations based on guessing in practice could not always match owners' perceptions. Although guessing and intersubjectivity played a central part for employees to understand the owner, incorrect guesses were unavoidable. Once misinterpretation happened, this would give rise to negative effects upon both workers' and employers' experiences. Misunderstanding created difficulties for employees to experience their work and for the owner to conduct labour management. Conflicts and tensions would take place between the two parties as a result.

Trust Difference

As indicated in the last section, Firm U's owner was originally from Tianjin, a northern city in China, where people speak Mandarin. Teng, the kitchen assistant, was from Tianjin as well. On one occasion, I had a discussion with Teng about the extent of the owner's trust in him. Teng told me:

> We are from the same place. He trusts me a lot. I can feel that.

I asked him:

> How about them (Cantonese speaking staff)?

Teng said with scorn:

> What do you think of this? It's for sure that the owner does not trust them. You know what? About a week ago, I told him I needed to be off the karaoke duty for a period to take rests. Yi soon introduced one of his friends to the owner as my replacement. On the day when the man did the trial, the owner texted me asking me to keep an eye on the numbers of drinks the customers ordered. He told me that they were from Guangdong, so he just could not trust them. After the trial, the owner had a conversation with me, expressing that he would not want to have the karaoke managed by that guy. He hoped that I could continue to manage the karaoke. I finally agreed.
>
> Anyway, we are both from Tianjin. I know he trusts me, and I would not cheat him. They are all southerners, speaking Cantonese. He (the owner) just simply does not trust them.

Yi's description indicated that the owner had low trust towards Cantonese speaking workers. The distrust from the owner of Cantonese speakers also was captured by me on one occasion. When Firm U re-opened after refurbishment, the front area manager was Zha. There were three kitchen workers: Yi, Dong and a pot washer from Portugal. Zha, Yi and Dong were all Cantonese speakers from Guangdong province.

Dong normally had his day off on Tuesdays. On a Monday afternoon, Dong had not appeared until around 12:20 PM. I asked Yi what happened to Dong. Yi told me that his 2-month baby had caught a high temperature so he would not come. On Tuesday, Dong took his day off as usual. He came to work on Wednesday. On Wednesday evening, I received a text message from Yi asking me whether I could work on Thursday (I regularly took my day off on Thursdays) because Dong's baby was still in a condition of high temperature. For that week, Dong took two more days off.

On Saturday, the owner came to collect revenues. He arrived at around 9:50 PM. After arrival, he invited everybody to have a hot pot with him. Yi and Dong politely declined because they would like to leave at 10 PM when the shift finished. Because the kitchen work was already done, I started to eat with the owner. About ten minutes later, Zha gave a slip of paper to the owner, telling him that it was the summary of the working hours for each worker this week. After Zha had left, the owner had another look at the paper and asked me:

How many days did Dong miss this week?

'Three days', answered I. After hearing that, he expressed that he knew this and added:

The kitchen is now managed by them (Cantonese speakers). If you find anything suspicious, tell me.

I did not know how many days Zha wrote on the slip. One thing was clear—due to the regular absence of the owner, the restaurant was entirely managed by Cantonese speaking workers, including the front area manager and the chefs. In a situation like this, there was much scope for cheating (see next chapter for further discussion). The owner's words to me explicitly expressed that he had little trust in Cantonese speaking workers. The distrust from the owner of Cantonese speaking workers led him to ask me, a Mandarin speaker, for double-check.

As mentioned earlier in this chapter, two British-born Chinese worked in Firm D. Zoe was a Mandarin speaker. I discussed the problem in communication between her and Kate in the previous section of this chapter. Janet was the other one. Unlike Zoe, Janet was a Cantonese speaker. Having worked with Janet for a while, I began to realise that Janet was the only part-time worker who had access to the till, and she was also the only Cantonese speaking worker in the front area. In other words, none of the other part-time workers were allowed to use the till, and they were all Mandarin speaking workers.

I one day asked Janet whether she had noticed the difference. Janet answered yes and said to me:

> She (the owner) does not trust them (Mandarin speaking workers). One day, it was me and Cui working on the evening shift. Because there was one table of English customers, I went to serve them, leaving Cui to manage the till. When Kate arrived, she directly walked into the counter and asked Cui to stop taking orders and go out of the counter area. When I was back to the counter, Kate said to me:
>
>> You need to take charge of ordering. How can you leave her to do this? If you would like her to use the till, you need to stand beside her and supervise her.

Kate's distrust of Mandarin speaking staff was also identified by Jack. Jack indeed did not quite like Janet. He thought Janet was always lazy. Furthermore, Janet had arguments with both Zoe and Cui, while Zoe and Cui were Jack's friends. One day before the lunch shift started, Jack had a check of condiments on each table. He found that the chilli and soy sauce bottles on many tables were empty. He then said to me:

> Look, they are all empty. Janet had yesterday's dinner shift. This meant that she did nothing. I don't know why Kate fancies her that much.

I said:

> And it feels that only Janet can gain Kate's trust. It seems that they (Mandarin speaking workers) are not allowed to use the till.

Jack replied:

> She doesn't trust them at all. They are not allowed to touch the till.

The above data illustrated that owners showed an obvious preference in trusting staff from their background. Firm U's owner was a Mandarin speaker. Even though he could speak fluent Cantonese, there was little trust from him towards Cantonese speaking workers. Firm D's owner was a Cantonese speaker. Under her management, only the Cantonese speaking girl could get trusted. Mandarin speaking workers simply were believed to be untrustworthy. The assumptions and prejudices of the two owners largely shaped their attitudes towards labour from a different background. Labour management was practised by the owners differently in relation to workers from different groups.

Inter-Group Conflicts

Two weeks into my research in Firm U, there were six employees in the kitchen: three Cantonese speaking chefs: Wen, Pian and Yi, and three Mandarin speaking kitchen assistants: Teng, Teng's wife and me. Although all of these three Cantonese speaking chefs could speak fluent Mandarin, communication between Cantonese speaking workers and Mandarin speaking workers was limited. Furthermore, because Cantonese speaking workers held the managerial positions in the kitchen, their attitudes towards Mandarin speakers, as Teng and Teng's wife believed, were not always friendly.

I once discussed this with Teng. He said:

> It was impossible for us to get along with them. They never want to have a close relationship with us. They are from the South while we are from the North.

During this initial stage, the Mandarin group and the Cantonese group were separated from each other. However, there were no direct conflicts between group members at this stage. This was largely because there was a clear hierarchy between Mandarin speaking workers and Cantonese speaking workers during this period. The dominant position for Cantonese speaking employees as chefs over Mandarin speaking employees as kitchen assistants gave them the power to dictate the relationship.

After a short while, both Wen and Pian left. Yi became the only Cantonese speaking chef, with Teng, Teng's wife and Juan as the Mandarin speaking kitchen workers. Although Yi took the managerial position of the kitchen, having lost his partners, Yi experienced challenges from Mandarin speaking workers. Direct conflicts occurred.

Juan one day arrived at around 12:10 PM, ten minutes late to work. After arriving, he began to cook for himself as he usually did. Having finished lunch, he turned on his tablet and started to watch. Yi was standing beside him, chopping beef. It seemed that Yi had some words with him. Juan suddenly spoke to Yi loudly:

> If you would like me to do something, just tell me directly, okay?

Yi answered:

> Don't you know what you should do? Is it always necessary for me to remind you?

Juan replied:

> It wouldn't be difficult to tell me what I should do, would it?

Yi said:

> We've been working as chefs for years. Don't you understand that the basic implicit understanding of being a chef is self-discipline?

Yuan still sat there, saying:

> But I'm not a self-disciplined person.

Yi mumbled some words and grabbed a cigarette leaving the kitchen. Their argument attracted Teng's attention. He came over to me and told me that Juan and Yi several days ago had another quarrel. The conflict on that occasion had been more intense. It was because they had different ideas on how to stir-fry a dish. Yi would like Juan to use his method, the way used by Southern chefs. However, Juan insisted that the dish should not be cooked in that way and finally ignored Yi's instruction. As Teng recalled, Yi finally threw the kitchen knife onto the cutting board and left.

Conflicts were not just between Juan and Yi; Teng and Yi also had direct conflicts. One day when Teng was cooking skewers, Yi went over to ask him whether he added extra salt into the seasoning. Teng said:

> There is no need to add extra salt. It is already salty enough.

After hearing this, Yi's face turned suddenly, and he said to Teng:

> I told you we had changed the way of marinating meat. The amount of salt is reduced when marinating the meat. You need to add extra salt into the seasoning.

However, Teng reacted strongly:

> I told you this is enough. Putting salt into the seasoning would make it too salty.

It seemed that Yi realised Teng would not follow his instruction. Yi did not say one more word and continued to do his work.

One day after we had finished dinner, only Teng, his wife and I were still at the table. Teng told me that the owner would come tomorrow. I asked him how he knew this. Teng said:

> He texted me this afternoon. He said he would come tomorrow to sort out some problems. He always texts me to get the latest information about the restaurant, asking me questions like how the kitchen is going, how the front area is going and how the karaoke is going.

I asked him:

> Does Yi know that he (the owner) will come tomorrow?

Teng said:

> How can I know this? But you just don't tell him the owner regularly texts me to update the kitchen conditions. He (the owner) may also text him as well. But don't let him know that he regularly sends me messages.

As mentioned above, Teng in the beginning already realised that there was a gap between the two groups of workers. Because Cantonese speaking chefs had the dominant position, there was not an explicit struggle between the two groups of workers. Due to the departure of Wen and Pian, Yi was separated from the other Mandarin speaking workers. Yi lost the dominant power to control the remaining Mandarin speaking workers. The latent tension between these two groups of people began to develop openly. This was why both Yi and Juan, and Yi and Teng had conflicts during this stage. As latent tension already developed into direct conflicts between Yi, as a Cantonese speaking worker, and Teng, as a Mandarin speaking worker, it was important to identify how they perceived each other to understand the hostility between them.

Chapter 4 mentioned that during the refurbishment period, on the day when Teng failed to negotiate with the owner for his stay, we had dinner that evening. Teng told me of recent progress in Firm U and analysed what led to his dismissal:

> It was not until today that I understand why he (the owner) did not retain me. Yi already found a few kitchen workers for him, at least two. One of them was to replace her (Teng pointed at his wife) to wash pots. Yi told me that the owner invited them to have dinner a couple of days ago. You know what? Two days ago, when I went to clean the karaoke,

I saw the owner was talking with three guys in the restaurant, including Yi. The other two must have been the ones Yi found for kitchen work.

Damn it! Yi must have already collaborated with the owner. The owner was shit as well. It is for sure that Yi asked the owner to dismiss us so that he could introduce people from Taishan (the city in Guangdong province, where most Cantonese speaking chefs originally came from). It must be like this. Once he has got his friends, it would give them the chances to do everything without being known by the owner.

Although most of Teng's conclusions were largely based on his guess, this clearly revealed his hatred towards Yi. He attributed his dismissal to Yi's trick. Teng's dissatisfaction at Yi even developed into hatred towards the whole group of Cantonese speaking workers. He believed that once Yi got rid of him, Cantonese speaking workers could fully take advantage of their unique ethnic tie.

Yi's perception about this case was also captured by me after Firm U re-opened. As analysed above, the two groups of workers had little communication at work. As a result, I had a relatively distant relationship with Yi in the beginning. However, our relationship improved during the refurbishment period. This was mainly because of two reasons. First, as a researcher, I understood that I must not engage the workplace conflicts. Unlike other Mandarin speaking workers, I followed the rules and Yi's instructions during my fieldwork. Second, cleaning was purely physical input, without any skills required. I worked diligently to complete every task Yi allocated to me. Gradually, I could identify that Yi was pleased to talk with me. Our talks were later not only limited to work-related issues. He began to talk about his personal life, such as his early experiences of working as a kitchen assistant in Newcastle and his marriage. Having noticed the change of Yi's attitudes towards me, I finally conducted a detailed discussion with Yi in the first week after Firm U re-opened. It was around Yi's experience during the decoration period and his perceptions of Teng's departure. Yi said:

They always had their own ideas, and they were extremely lazy. They were also unsatisfied with their wages. You know what? When I started my work in England, I earned £200 a week. It was not until the fifth year that my wage rose to £230 a week. How about them? He earned £300 a week; his wife earned £300 a week, as well. He also took the karaoke job. That was a lot.

Moreover, he was always angry with me. Doesn't he know his position? He was just a worker. It felt as if he was the owner. He has been in a bad temper towards me. One day the plumber came to fix the sink.

I forgot to mop the floor that evening. On the next day when we met in the kitchen, he deliberately said: 'Shit! Who cleaned the floor yesterday? Water is everywhere'. He then threw the plug to me. Damn it! He was furious with me just due to such a tiny thing. Who did he think he was? And his wife, last time I asked her to clean those containers. You know what? I had already taken the containers out and put them into the sink. She just put them back, and she was angry with me. She was the one recruited to wash plates. She just refused to do that. Listen, in the second week of my arrival, Pian wanted to let them go. If he was not in charge of the karaoke, they would have already gone. I tolerated them so much. I just could not bear them anymore.

Furthermore, they were illegal workers. I have a UK passport. I can work anywhere. Can they? You know what? If I had called the immigration office, they would have been forcefully ejected back to China. I have been so kind to them. They thought they were treated unfairly by me. Look at what he did later on, wearing a jacket, walking around the kitchen at 4 PM and asking whether the meal was ready. Fuck off. It was working time. If he was in another restaurant, he would have been immediately fired.

I said:

But you never mentioned this before. It felt like you were so kind to them.

Yi replied:

I was. Working here is the easiest job in the world. Don't you think I wouldn't want to stay here? I just think we are all Chinese. It was tough for them to work abroad. I therefore decided to leave and let them stay. They believed I stabbed them in the back.

When discussing the chefs' negotiation power in Chapter 4, I mentioned that Yi finally decided to stay because the owner promised to give him £200 per week during the decoration period and raised his weekly wage from £450 to £480. Although Yi claimed that the reason why he would like to leave Firm U was that he would like to let Teng and his wife work in Firm U, it was surely not the deciding factor. Yi's descriptions expressed his strong dissatisfaction at Teng and his wife. Their unwillingness to follow his orders, their laziness and their bad attitudes all caused Yi's hatred.

Yi's hostility towards Teng was also recognised by the owner. Chapter 4 when analysing the negotiation power for kitchen assistants mentioned that

I once conducted a discussion with the owner aiming to explore his percep-tions about Teng's negotiation for a wage rise. The owner discussed his opinion from a labour market point of view. In the discussion, I also asked him how he understood the conflict between Yi and Teng. He answered:

> It is a long-lasting problem. Both of them had talked to me about the other's problem. However, as an owner, I've got to make the decision. Let me just ask you. One is the head chef, and the other is a kitchen assistant. Who would you pick if you were me? He (Yi) not only had a conflict with Teng. His hatred was widespread to any non-Taishanese. They (Taishanese) are all like this.

After Teng's dismissal, Zha, the front area manager, started to manage kara-oke. One day when it was approaching 10 PM, I found that Yi was still on the upper floor serving karaoke customers. I went to ask him why he was still working. He said:

> Zha is not coming today. He told me that he had done three consecutive night shifts. He said he was too tired. He would like me to do today's shift. I agreed. I have known his parents for a long time. We are all Tais-han brothers. I've got to help him. You know what? Teng previously sometimes also asked me whether I could help him to do a few shifts. I never agreed. Why would I help him?

Up until this point, the analysis in this section has illustrated the struggles and conflicts between Mandarin speaking workers and Cantonese speak-ing workers. Conflicts also existed within each sub-group. For the group of Cantonese speakers, I did not notice obvious conflicts between them throughout my fieldwork. The reason would be that most of the Canton-ese speaking workers were from Guangdong province so that they share the common language and culture. By contrast, Mandarin speaking work-ers were heterogeneous from different provinces. Although Teng and Juan were both Mandarin speaking workers, Teng was from Tianjin municipality while Juan was from Jiangsu province. Juan and Teng had direct conflicts several times during the period of my fieldwork.

It was a busy evening on Saturday. Both Teng and I had not stopped even for one second since the start of the evening shift. When Juan finished a stir-fry order, he came to chat with me about his plan to go back to China. Teng said to him:

> If I were in China now, I would kill you with no doubt (Teng expressed his dissatisfaction at Juan's laziness).

Juan replied:

> Come, you can kill me now. There is no need saying that if you were in China. Just come, use the chopper. I will give you a surprise.

They then looked at each other with scorn. Later that evening, after Teng and I had finished all the skewer orders, we sat down chatting to each other. Teng said to me:

> We've never experienced so many orders on one single shift, have we? I'm exhausted. Well, this is because people in the kitchen are not united, unwilling to work for each other (Teng alluded to Juan).

Having heard Teng's words, Juan reacted immediately:

> It seems as if you did everything. It feels like once you leave, the restaurant would shut down immediately.

Before Juan went back to China, I had a detailed discussion with him. The conversation aimed to explore two issues: one was about how regulations influenced both owner-managers' and employees' choices (this will be discussed in the next chapter), and the other was about how he experienced his work during the period of working in Firm U. Juan said:

> There are too many annoying things here, too many, although there are only a few people. Everybody would like to discuss gossip behind others' backs. But I don't care at all. Moreover, if I feel good, I may do something beyond my responsibility. If not, I only do my job. If food is deteriorating or smelly, that's none of my business.
>
> I have been here (UK) for so long. I've never met a person from Tianjin municipality (where Teng was from) with good quality. They are all shit, saying one thing and doing another. Several days ago, the owner came to have a chat with me, saying that 'Juan, you need to clean the kitchen with them'. I don't want to explain to him. I know they have reported me to the owner. I don't care. As long as I was paid each week, everything is fine.
>
> It's so annoying working here. Everybody thinks they have done more work than others. It feels like the restaurant is reliant upon them. To be honest, Teng and his wife made me feel extremely unpleasant. You were there that day, right? When I finished my lunch and gave the bowl to his wife, she said to me: 'You don't pay so you wash for yourself'. How could she possibly speak like this? So, can I say, 'You

don't pay so you are not allowed to eat the meal cooked by me'? That's disgusting. Furthermore, are they really unconscious of their illegal identities? They are illegal workers. As illegal workers, how can they behave like this? Absolutely absurd.

Although both Teng and Juan spoke Mandarin and came from China's northern cities, this did not mean that they could easily work together in the UK context. Direct conflicts were frequent between them. Juan's words expressed his hatred towards Teng and Teng's wife. Just like Teng's antagonism to Cantonese speakers and Yi's antagonism to Mandarin speakers, Juan also extended his antagonism towards Teng to the wider population— people from Tianjin municipality. These deep-rooted perceptions prevented them from working harmoniously and significantly shaped their day-to-day behaviours on the shop floor, which revealed the internal struggles between multi-cultural workforces in the ethnic Chinese restaurant sector.

Conclusions

This chapter discussed the dynamics between multi-cultural workforces in the two restaurants. In the specific context of the ethnic Chinese restaurant sector, it mainly consisted of three groups: Mandarin speaking workers, Cantonese speaking workers and British-born Chinese. Existing research in exploring employment relations in ethnic small firms rarely discussed the heterogeneous character within ethnic groups. Analysis in this chapter did not treat the co-ethnicity as a homogeneous group. The aim was to reveal how this ethnic mix influenced employment relationships and management practices.

Due to the different languages being used, there had been significant communication problems between different groups of workers. Wapshott and Mallett (2013) demonstrated the importance of intersubjectivity in shaping patterns of adaptation and accommodation between owners and workers in ambiguity-intensive small professional service firms. The concept of intersubjectivity reflected the unspoken side of communication and tacit understandings. In this context, due to the language barrier and the communication problem, employees frequently drew on the perception of the owners' value or interests. Guessing played a central role in facilitating the mutual adjustment process. However, because employees' assessments of employers' perceptions were based on their intersubjective assumptions under different situations, it was inevitable that mis-interpretation existed. The process of workplace control would be seriously influenced once workers failed to correctly capture owner-managers' intentions. The intersubjective guessing arising from the language barrier, therefore, had important consequences for the work organisation and employment relations in the ethnic Chinese restaurant sector. It on the one hand reflected the nature of informal accommodation in small firms (Marlow, 2005), and on the other hand led to tensions and conflicts between owner-managers and workers.

Owners' trust towards workers from different groups was significantly different within the context of multi-cultural workforces. Firm D's owner had a Cantonese background. As a result, only one part-time worker with a Cantonese background was allowed to use the till. Mandarin background workers were not allowed to use the till due to her low trust in them. Firm U's owner had a Mandarin background. As a result, he did not fully trust anybody who had a Cantonese background. Under the multi-cultural working environment, the assumptions and prejudices of the two owners largely shaped their attitudes towards labour from different backgrounds. Labour management was practised by the owners differently when treating workers from different groups.

The central focus of this chapter was the conflict between members from different cultural groups and regions. This mainly referred to the conflict between Cantonese speakers from the Southern area and Mandarin speakers from the Northern area. Empirical data illustrated that there had been substantial hatred and hostility between Cantonese speaking workers and Mandarin speaking workers. These two groups of workers were reluctant to work together, with limited communication while working. Without the willingness to tolerate and support each other, there engaged in frequent conflicts and struggles. Conflicts between Mandarin speakers from different regions were also significant. Tensions among workers at the shop floor reflected their deep-rooted antagonism of each group towards another. Workplace behaviours and shop floor dynamics were considerably influenced in such a context.

6 Interaction Between Informality and Ethnicity

Chapter 1 has discussed the importance of an understanding of the interaction between informality and ethnicity in shaping workplace behaviours and management practices in ethnic minority small firms. The employment of family members eased management pressures and facilitated informal control strategies (Ram ct al., 2000; Aldrich and Cliff, 2003). By employing ethnic female workers, owners could intensify their control and carry out low-pay strategies in labour management (Ram, 1994). Moreover, as ethnic small firms largely competed within low-profit added sectors, the introduction of NMW and WTR put extra pressures on these firms and forced some of them to engage in illegal practices (Jones et al., 2006).

This chapter analyses how informality interacting with ethnicity shaped employment relations in the context of the ethnic Chinese restaurant sector. The first section discusses the informal management system in the two restaurants and the implications of employment relationships. Section 2 discusses how management and employees reacted to a variety of laws and regulations. Different patterns of employment relations during the adaptation process will be analysed.

Workplace Control and the Dynamics of Negotiation

Informal Practices in the Two Firms

Staff Recruitment

The manner in which employees were recruited to the two firms could be largely characterised by the use of informal networks. The 'grapevine' recruitment was regarded as the most simple and cost-effective method for recruiting both chefs and front area workers. In Firm D, Jack, the front area manager, altogether introduced four of his friends, including me. Firm D throughout my research only recruited one chef, who was recommended by another chef. In Firm U, all of the part-time front area workers before the refurbishment were friends of Ming, the front area manager. They knew each other when they previously worked in another restaurant. For Firm U's kitchen staff, after the couple workers had left, the head chef Wen introduced both Yi and Pian, his two former colleagues. After the refurbishment, Yi, as the head chef, brought in Zha, the front area manager, and Dong, the other chef.

In both sites, for chefs and front area staff who were introduced by existing staff, they would get employed straightaway. Indeed, both owners encouraged employees to call their friends and acquaintances to work for them. Most of the chefs who were introduced by existing staff had previously spent years working in ethnic Chinese restaurants in Sheffield. They surely had basic skills. Owners believed that this could hugely reduce uncertainties for picking up workers, especially for kitchen staff.

Training

There was no training for new chefs in both restaurants. The chefs who were recruited were 'ready-made' as they had been working in the Chinese restaurant sector for years. Once they were recruited, they started their work immediately. For kitchen assistants and front area workers, 'training' basically started from the three-hour trial period before recruited. They were taught some basic tasks, and the working environment was introduced. Once recruited, they started their work with on-the-job training. There was no clear time to differentiate 'training' and 'working'. As a worker became more skilled, they had less 'training' and more 'working'. As labour costs comprised a large proportion of total revenues for these businesses, cost-saving strategies dominated many aspects of management. It was therefore difficult for owner-managers to invest in training. With the application of on-the-job training, owners could save a large amount of labour costs. On-the-job training was also sufficient for front area workers and kitchen assistants to acquire basic abilities.

Supervision

In Firm D, although the owner worked together with employees as co-workers, there was a clear hierarchy and division between them. The method of close employee supervision was generally applied. Without clear rules and policies in guiding the management process, performance appraisal and supervision were managed based on Kate's judgement. In Firm U, when the owner was absent from the site, there was a desire for the front area manager and the head chef to create a harmonious environment with less intense supervision. Once the owner appeared, it became relatively intense. He would point out everything that he thought was improperly done and expect employees to accept his requirements.

Pay Arrangements

Pay levels in these two firms were initially set by owners. Pay increases were basically a product of individual bargaining. As discussed in Chapter 4, the negotiation power for a pay rise for kitchen assistants and front area staff was weak. No kitchen assistant or front area workers during my fieldwork successfully negotiated a pay rise. By contrast, chefs' dominant labour market position gave them a large scope to negotiate for their interests. Owners generally were afraid of direct conflict with chefs due to the short supply of skilled chefs from the labour market. Chefs had the power to resist managerial strategies and work on wage-effort bargaining. For example, Yi successfully bargained for a pay rise during Firm U's refurbishment period.

Staff Exit

Under a turbulent environment, the staff turnover rate was significantly high in these two firms. Because part-time front area workers were all students, a voluntary departure from them was frequent with different reasons, such as doing revision for exams. For full-time workers, the only tacit rule in both sites concerning voluntary staff exit was that workers should apply for leaving one week ahead. It was simply an oral application. If the owner would like to keep the worker, it then went into the negotiation stage over pay or any other related issues. The involuntary exit was also frequent. For kitchen assistants and part-time front area workers, as discussed in Chapter 4, if an owner would like to sack them, they generally had no choice but to be compliant. Dismissal for these two groups of workers was largely dominated by the owners' perceptions. By contrast, there had been no dismissal for a single chef in both restaurants throughout my research.

Dynamics of Informality and the Negotiated Order

When I started my fieldwork in Firm D, Jack had two days off a week, on Thursdays and Saturdays. A full-time worker normally could only have one day off a week. The reason why Jack had an extra day off was that he had a college course on Thursdays in Birmingham. After he had completed the course, Jack regularly took one day off on Saturdays. However, it seemed that Jack had been used to having two days off. He one day complained that he felt exhausted by working six days a week. He told me that he would like to ask Kate for one day off on weekdays. On Sunday when the roster for the next week was released, I found that Jack did not have a shift on Thursday. I asked him how he negotiated with Kate so that he could secure a day off on weekdays. Jack told me:

> Um, she did not agree in the beginning. I just insisted that I was too tired by working six days. It made me exhausted. She hesitated for a moment and said to me: 'Okay. Okay. If you are too tired and would like to take two days off, that's all right. However, you need to work until 8 PM on the other days (Jack's shifts normally ended at 7 PM)'. I accepted her bargain. You know what, I know I can get allowed to take one more day off. Haha.

In the final week of my fieldwork in Firm D, I told Jack I would finish my work by the end of the week. Jack thought for a short while and said to me:

> It may be sensible for me to reduce my shifts, as well. I do not even have time to exercise. Probably being part-time from now on. I will speak to her (Kate).

I didn't know what Jack said to Kate and how he argued with her, but the fact was that Jack had another day off on Monday the next week. After the two negotiations, Jack ended with three days off a week rather than one day off.

Having completed the extensive fieldwork in Firm D, I one day went to find Jack to get updates on the restaurant. Jack spoke to me:

> I am so tired now. I have been working for two consecutive weeks, without having one day off. It's now during the exam period. They (part-time workers) are all preparing for their exams. Kate did not want to recruit any new staff only for this short period. If I did not work, there would be no one working here. She talked to me several times and wanted me to work for her. I finally agreed. But I am telling you, I am absolutely exhausted now, and this will probably continue for one more week.

As Jack was a full-time worker, the labour market enabled him the strong negotiation power. He frequently engaged in direct bargaining with Kate for his interests. Later, in the face of a temporary departure of all part-time workers, Firm D encountered a crisis. Under a situation like this, mutual dependence and social proximity between Jack and Kate came into play and interacted with the external environment in shaping their behaviours. The accommodation between Jack and Kate was continuous and contingent upon diverse situations. Orders were subject to constant informal negotiation between them. Their experiences were influenced by a range of factors, both internally and externally.

The above case was one of the examples demonstrating how the order in the two firms was negotiated with the influence of both external structures and internal variables. Analysis in Chapter 3 and Chapter 4 illustrated how the demand fluctuation and the labour market shaped the management control strategies with a process of continuous bargaining between owner-managers and workers. Additionally, ethno-cultural influences such as the conflicts between different groups of workers also significantly affected the shop floor dynamics. The dynamics of relations between Mandarin speaking workers and Cantonese speaking workers were heavily influenced by hatred and antagonism on a day-to-day basis, which was elaborated in Chapter 5. Management practices and workplace relations in the two restaurants were shaped by the interaction between structural factors and internal forces with the bargained nature.

Scope for Cheating and Fiddles

Personal Cheating

As noted earlier, apart from being a kitchen assistant in Firm U, Teng also had the task of managing karaoke. As long as there were karaoke customers, Teng had to continue to serve them after completing his shift. Firm U had only one key. Teng always held the key because he needed to lock the door after he had finished his karaoke job. In the beginning, when there were no karaoke customers, Teng left together with other employees at 10 PM. Gradually, everybody was used to Teng staying in the restaurant after work due to his karaoke task, although there would be no karaoke customers on a particular day. One day when there were no karaoke customers, everybody left at 10 PM as usual. I waited for Teng to lock the door and leave together. However, having seen that everybody had left, Teng locked the door from inside and went back to the kitchen, telling me that he would cook some food and take it home. The tacit understanding was that Teng would manage the karaoke after work so it was no problem for him to continue staying in the restaurant. This therefore gave him the chance to cheat the system due to a lack of supervision under the informal management structure. I later found that it became a regular activity for him to cook after work.

Chapter 4 mentioned that Firm D had a custom of sharing tips between full-time waiters and the owner. There was a bucket at the counter used for tips. One day when Jack and I worked on the evening shift, Jack suddenly said to me angrily:

> Shit! I will no longer put tips into the bucket. A long time ago, I knew that she (Kate) rarely put tips into the bucket. She put all tips into the till; the till was her personal property. Although this has been annoying, I have been putting tips into the bucket. I just simply would like to stick to the rule. She received £5 tips this afternoon. I stood beside her. She put the note into the till straightaway in front of me. Fuck off! I will never leave any tips into the bucket. The customer just left £5 tips. It now belongs to me!

Personal cheating in the two restaurants was largely attributed to the absence of effective supervision in these two firms, especially in Firm U. Due to the lack of effective supervision, employees had space to manipulate rules and modify control. For Teng's case, it was more a matter of taking advantage of the informal management structure. By contrast, the fiddle practised by Jack was a type of workplace resistance to management. It was expressed as the dissatisfaction of managerial control.

Cheating by Informal Connection

In Firm D, apart from being a kitchen assistant, another task for Huo was to deliver takeaway. One day when Huo had his day off, Kate asked me to deliver takeaway together with Nick, the male owner. When we came back after having delivered a few orders, I was told by Kate that there were some new orders waiting to be delivered. Kate asked me to wait for a short while until they were ready. Jack then went towards me and said:

> Lewis, my friend ordered one of these. It was the order from the Power One (the property name). When you give the food to him, you don't take his money. Nick never gets off the car when delivering. I asked my friend to wait inside the building. You just go in and give the food to him. That's fine. Nick never checks the money. When you come back, just give the money to me. Both Kate and Nick cannot know this. That would be no problem at all.

About ten minutes later, when the chef had finished cooking, I began to pack the food. At the same time, Jack was having a discussion with Kate about the end of his shift. Because there was one order from the building he lived in, he expressed that he would like to deliver and go home directly.

Kate agreed. It was Jack who delivered finally, although I did not ask Jack whether he finally did not collect money from his friend.

One day when Cui, Jack and I worked on the evening shift, Cui suddenly told Jack she was really hungry. Jack expressed that he was hungry as well. After a short discussion, they picked one dish they would like to eat. Jack then wrote the dish on an order sheet, marking that it was from a table of customers who added this dish, and he gave it to kitchen staff. When the dish was ready, they began to eat at the counter. With this little trick, they did not pay for the dish.

At the beginning of this chapter when discussing the informal labour management practices in the two firms, it mentioned that the informal network was widely used as the recruitment technique because this way was efficient and cost-effective. However, it worked as a double-edged sword here. Cui and I were both recruited by Jack. As his friends, we were trusted by him, but trust arising from the informal personal connection allowed employees to cheat the system and created scope for fiddles.

Cheating by Intergroup Relations

Ming, the front area manager in Firm U before the refurbishment, started her work only a few days ahead of me. She was recruited by the owner to replace a former front area manager, Jemma, who was sacked due to deliberately working with karaoke staff to give false information about the revenue.

Firm U's karaoke had different types of set menus. For each type, they were composed of different drinks depending on how much the set menu was, and for each set menu, three hours of free singing was included. If customers would like to continue singing, they needed to pay an additional £30 per hour. Because there was no computer-based order system, orders were recorded manually. According to the rule, a karaoke worker was required to write down what type of set menu was ordered and how many additional hours added. Because the CCTV to cover the karaoke counter had been broken, there was no supervision to the upper floor karaoke area. The owner could only check the revenue based on the order notes written by workers. This left the scope for workers to submit false information.

Before Teng was in charge of karaoke, it had been managed by two part-time employees. After they had been sacked, the two former part-time workers regularly played in Firm U's karaoke as customers. They gradually got familiar with Teng and they later told Teng the truth about why they were dismissed, which nobody had ever known before. Teng one day told me:

> Now, I completely understand how they collaborated with the front area manager to cheat. They told me everything yesterday.

As you know, there was no supervision for karaoke, no CCTV coverage. Everybody knew that it was easy to take advantage of this loophole. When I noted down the order yesterday, they (the two sacked former karaoke staff) came over and suggested to me to write the false note and even taught me how this could be properly done without danger of being identified. They said:

> The thing is that it is impossible to cheat on the set menus because he (the owner) knew the number of drinks in stock. However, he would never know how many extra hours a room of customers added. Suppose that they add three hours. If you note down two hours, you will get £30; if you note down one hour, you will get £60, and if you note down none, all the £90 would belong to you. This is exactly what we did. If you note down the real hours they add, as you are doing now, you can never take the advantage. He (the owner) later seemed to realise this and asked Jemma to supervise. However, he did not know that Jemma and we were in the same camp. She covered for us, and we shared the money. You know what? Our weekly was set as £400. By doing this, we could earn at least £700 a week by using these tricks. Sadly, a pot washer heard our talk on one occasion and reported this to the owner.

The intergroup cheating in Firm D was even more significant. On a Friday evening, both Kate and Nick (the couple owners) left for their friend's birthday. It was Jack and I on the shift. A man with a child came in and walked straight into the kitchen. Jack told me that they were Kang's (a chef in Firm D) husband and daughter. They ordered some food and began their meal. Because the owners were absent, Kang later went out to eat with them. After they had finished, Kang's husband went to the counter preparing to pay. Kang followed him to the counter and said to Jack with a smile:

> It has been paid.

Jack smiled back. Kang's husband and daughter left without actually paying for the meal.

The similar case also happened to Huo (one of Firm D's kitchen assistants). It was another day when the owners were absent. They went to a Chinese party in the afternoon. In the evening, Huo's two friends came to have a meal. After they had finished, Huo went out speaking to Jack:

> I know you are kind. Everything is fine. It's okay.

Jack clearly understood what he meant. He nodded his head and smiled at Huo. Huo's friends left after paying nothing.

After Huo had gone into the kitchen, I asked Jack whether this type of 'free meal' always happened. Jack answered:

> Yes, whenever they (the owners) were not on-site, they would invite their friends to come for meals. It was annoying indeed.

I asked Jack:

> But you wouldn't tell them (the owners), would you? Otherwise, it is impossible for them to do this.

Jack replied:

> No, they (kitchen staff) know I wouldn't tell them (Kate and Nick). This is not my business. Although I don't like the way they did it, I wouldn't report this to them. Furthermore, I'm taking over the business in a few months. I need them to work for me. I just don't want to irritate them, at least for now.

The informally organised intergroup relationship was able to modify and resist a series of managerial control efforts to create scope for fiddles and cheating on the shop floor. By exploring the intergroup cheating, it further advanced the understanding of how workplace behaviours could be shaped under the informal management structure. Furthermore, fiddles conducted by intergroup connection demonstrated the lack of solidarity between owners and workers in the ethnic Chinese restaurant sector, which reflected the strong link to ethnicity.

Laws and Regulations

The NMW Breach

During the period of my fieldwork from November 2014 to July 2015, the NMW for workers aged 21 years and over was £6.50 per hour; for those aged 18–20, it was £5.13; and for workers under 18, it was £3.79 per hour (NMW, 2015). Table 6.1 shows the hourly wage in the two firms for each type of employee during my research. The amount in the table for each worker's hourly wage was based on my discussion with them, although I was not able to verify these reports with reference to pay slips.

Table 6.1 The Hourly Wage Each Type of Worker Earned in the Two Firms

	Firm D	*Firm U*
Part-time front area workers	£5	£5
Full-time front area workers	£5.50	£5.70 and £6.70
Kitchen assistants	£5.50	£5
Chefs	between £7.50 and £8.30	between £7.50 and £8.30

According to the table, the pay level in the two firms for part-time front area employees was the same: £5 per hour. Because no employees under 18 ever worked in the two restaurants, this amount was definitely below the NMW level. Full-time front area workers were paid differently. The wage of Jack, Firm D's manager, was calculated based on an hourly rate. His hourly wage was £5.50. Ming, the initial manager in Firm U, was paid £340 a week. She worked ten hours a day, six days a week. This meant that her hourly wage was £5.70 per hour. Zha, the second manager in Firm U, was paid £400 a week. He also worked ten hours a day, six days a week, which meant that his hourly wage was £6.70 per hour.

The only kitchen assistant in Firm D was paid £330 per week, working ten hours a day, six days a week, which was equivalent to £5.50 per hour. Kitchen assistants in Firm U were all paid £300 per week, with the same amount of working time. Their hourly wage amounted to £5 per hour. Chefs in both sites were paid between £450 and £500 per week, which meant that their hourly wage was between £7.50 and £8.30.

Based on these numerical data, chefs' wages were over the NMW level. Given that no workers in these two firms were under 21 years of age, for the remaining workers except for Zha, their wages were all lower than the statutory minimum rate. After realising the widespread underpayment of the NMW, I once asked Yi whether the breach of the law was common in ethnic Chinese restaurants. Yi answered:

> This (the NMW) has nothing to do with us (Chinese restaurants). It's something to regulate British restaurants. I have been here so many years, working in several different places. No restaurant followed that rule.

I continued to ask:

> So, what decides workers' pay levels?

Yi said:

> The market. The market decides this. Look, all the part-time work-ers are now paid £5 per hour. It's the same everywhere. Some may

pay £5.50 if they like. Cantonese cuisine chefs were generally paid between £450 and £500 per week while Sichuan cuisine chefs were paid between £500 and £550 per week, or even higher. This is the current situation in Sheffield. The market determines wages.

According to Yi's description, the ethnic Chinese restaurant sector did not regard the NMW as a law to regulate them. Indeed, Firm D's owner shared a similar idea. In a discussion with Kate about the NMW, she said:

I know. I know the NMW. But I don't know the current level. You know, we don't measure the wage by that. There is a common recognition for wages in particular jobs. We would achieve an agreement before they decide to take a job. I tell them how much I'd like to pay them. If they agree, they take the job.

Although there was a tacit understanding of the wage level in the ethnic Chinese restaurant sector, the pay level by any means for most workers was lower than the NMW standard. A potential issue behind the alleged widespread violation of the law was that once workers were dismissed unfairly or felt unsatisfied with the business for any reason, they might report the NMW breach, which might result in the business being investigated. Given the potential danger of breaching the law, the practical labour management practices might constrain owner-managers' choices in sacking employees and their manners in treating employees, and employees' wage-bargaining power would also be enhanced. However, as Chapter 4 analysed, apart from chefs, other groups of workers had little negotiating power, especially when it came to the stage of dismissal. So, how should the contradiction be explained?

To answer this question, it was necessary to explore how the owner-managers perceived the violation, why owner-managers were confident that the low-pay practice would not cause any potential trouble to their businesses and why threatening to report the alleged violation would not enhance employees' negotiation power.

With these questions in mind, I once asked Kate whether she had any concern that employees might report the breach of the NMW. Kate said to me:

No. There is no need to worry about this. We would agree on the wage level before they start their work. For example, for those students (part-time front area workers), if they would like to work with £5 per hour, they take the job. It's the agreement made by both parties. Once they decide to work here, it means that they accept the offer. So, they won't report this. No one has ever done this before, kitchen staff and students. This never happens. It's not just me who pays their wages at this level. Every Chinese restaurant in Sheffield does the same. So, I'm not bothered.

According to the conversation, she did not worry about the possibility of being reported by employees. The confidence arose from her belief that it was an agreed exchange, and because there had been no previous incidents of employees reporting her to the authorities. However, Kate's words did not explain why employees would not report this, individually or collectively, even if the amount of wage was agreed beforehand and the same levels of wages were applied to every restaurant in Sheffield.

To explain why employees did not choose to report the NMW breach, and why they accepted a wage much lower than the NMW, I discussed the problems with many workers in the two restaurants. After these discussions, I realised that there were several factors that restrict employees' choices. The 'small Chinese community' was one of the constraints, as Yi explained:

> We can't. It's impossible for us to do this. This is a small community. Everyone (people in the Chinese restaurant sector) knows everyone. We work in different restaurants. Changing workplaces is rather normal. If somebody does this, nobody will employ him. That's for sure.

I continued to ask Yi:

> How about Wen (Wen previously worked in Firm U, and later found his own restaurant)? He has his own business now.

Yi said:

> Who knows how long his business could last? He is now working with two partners. I'm telling you. It's highly likely that they split up one day. Once this happens, he still needs to find a job. If he does this (reporting), who will employ him? No way.
>
> Furthermore, as I once told you, it's an agreement. I (an owner) can offer you that amount of money. If you (an employee) are happy with that, you choose to work; otherwise, you decline the offer. That's it.

Yi's words pointed out how the 'small community' limited workers' choices. If anybody did this, they would never be employed in Sheffield. However, for those who did not rely on the 'Sheffield Chinese community', such as part-time student workers or any worker who was leaving Sheffield, this might not be a constraint. But there was another factor that prevented employees from successfully reporting the violation—cash-in-hand payment. As all payment in these two restaurants was cash-in-hand, it was therefore unlikely to have 'proof' of the alleged widespread breach of the NMW regulations. Both Jack and Zha believed that it was impossible for an employee to report the violation successfully as long as the owner denied that he had ever employed the person. Jack explained this to me:

> No one would do this. I've never seen anybody doing this, although conflicts or even fighting once happened between Kate and former part-time workers. The owner can just simply refuse to admit that she has ever employed the worker.

Zha described:

> When I worked in Firm K, one day the city council sent two men to investigate the NMW violation. Firm K was reported for sure. They stayed there for two days, asking questions to employees. They finally got nothing. Nobody co-operated with them.

With these two reasons, informing an NMW violation was hardly achievable in Sheffield's restaurant sector. Based on my conversation with the participants, no restaurant had ever been caught paying workers under the NMW regulations. Furthermore, the violation of the NMW regulations in the two firms was not simply in the way of paying workers under the minimum level. According to workers' accounts, there was deliberate co-operation between owners and workers in cheating the system, which established some pay-related routines in the two firms.

As discussed in Chapter 5, the relationship between Yi and me improved a lot during the cleaning stage before Firm U re-opened. With our relationship becoming closer, Yi began to share more information with me:

> We only reported (to the tax authorities) working time from 24 hours to 30 hours a week. This meant that I worked as a part-time worker. We then collected subsidies from the government. It was about 40- or 50-something a week.

Because all the wages in the two firms were paid cash-in-hand, there was no way for the government to trace the real working hours. Once the owner and workers collaborated to report the false working hours, a worker might earn at least £40 a week according to Yi.

Chapter 5 mentioned that before Juan (the chef in Firm U) left for China, I had a detailed discussion with him. One theme was about his working experiences in Firm U, which was in relation to conflicts between different group members, and the other was about cheating the system. Given that I already knew how Yi took advantage of loopholes, I asked Juan whether he did this in the same way. Juan said:

> Not here. I only work here for two weeks. That's not a large amount. Anyway, I did the same when I was in London. I'm telling you. Every Chinese restaurant does the same thing. No Chinese restaurant exactly follows the law. That is something to regulate British restaurants.

Juan's description demonstrated that it was not a single case just for Yi. Reporting false working hours was widespread in ethnic Chinese restaurants in the UK. The cheating occurred not only in Sheffield, also in London (because Juan previously worked in London). Dong also confirmed the cheating.

As mentioned in Chapter 3, Dong was Yi's friend joining Firm U during the refurbishment. Having developed a good relationship with Dong, I one day discussed the problem of deliberately breaching the regulation with him. Dong told me:

> Yes, we all do the same. I've got two children. My wife needs to take care of them. So, I can get a little bit more. It (the subsidy) is more than £100 a week. My weekly wage is £450. The extra money for a month is equivalent to my one-week income. That's not bad. We make use of the loophole and get the money that belongs to us.

Zha, the front area manager in Firm U, also told me that this trick was used by all ethnic Chinese workers who hold a British passport. They completed the form as part-time workers, by only working 24 hours a week. These workers viewed this action as a legitimate way to use the loophole in the regulation to get extra money, despite it being illegal. That is why Dong claimed 'get the money that belongs to us'.

Furthermore, it is also necessary to note that the cheating was achieved with the owners' help. They helped employees provide false hours so they could work as 'part-time' workers. Previous chapters discussed different types of conflict and resistance between employers and employees. However, when facing the NMW violation, they co-operated to cheat the system with a tacit understanding of how to behave.

The WTR Breach

As mentioned in Chapter 5, all of the part-time front area workers were university students. According to the Working Time Regulations (2003), the Tier 4 visa for Chinese allows each student to work in the UK for a maximum of 20 hours per week during term time. However, the fact was that no workers and owners in the two firms took the regulation seriously. The arrangement of work for both parties never took the law as a reference.

After Firm U's re-decoration, there were only three regular part-time front area workers. All of them were Master's students. One of them worked five days a week with ten hours a day, including both the lunch shifts and the dinner shifts; another worked four days a week with also ten hours a day. This meant that they worked 50 and 40 hours a week respectively, which was far more than the limit stipulated by the regulation. The roster was developed based on a discussion between Zha and these part-time workers according to their requirements. The concern of WTR regulations was completely not involved.

In Firm D, the ignorance of the regulations relating to working hours was also obvious. When it was in the penultimate week of the first term, because two out of the three part-time workers had already completed their first-term classes, they decided not to come to work in the final week. Cui, as a result, became the only remaining part-time worker. Average shifts for a part-time worker per week were three to four shifts in Firm D. Due to the other two workers' temporary departure, Cui had ten shifts in the final week. Her working time during that week was over 30 hours.

Among all the part-time workers in the two restaurants, Jing was the only one who had ever worked in a British restaurant. I one day had a chat with her about her experience while working in that British restaurant, especially issues around the working hours. She told me:

> I worked there about over one month as a part-time waitress. The maximum hours I ever worked for a week were 18. They just did not allow me to work any longer. While, for us (Chinese restaurants), nobody paid attention to the regulation. Many even don't know it.

When I discussed with Kate whether she had any worry that students might report to the council about paying the wage below the minimum level, she even said:

> Nobody would do this. Moreover, they are students. They are not allowed to work that long. How can they report to the council?

Kate's words demonstrated that she understood the working time limit for a part-time worker. For each student, the law was clearly printed on their students' cards. However, the WTR regulation did not affect both owners and workers' choices too much.

The Health Act Breach

On the first day of my fieldwork in Firm U, having finished lunch, kitchen workers went back to the kitchen and began to smoke at the corner near the back door. If it were in China, it would be fine to smoke inside a restaurant in most places. According to the Health Act 2006 (Health Act, 2006), relating to health and safety in workplaces in England, it is illegal to smoke in all enclosed spaces. After smoking, they started their work. About two hours later, the head chef stopped working. He walked towards the corner and called another chef. They lit their cigarettes and smoked again. One week through my research, I even found that there was a 'smoking time'. The 'smoking time' took place regularly twice a day: after lunch and dinner. On each day when chefs finished lunch and dinner, they would gather together to smoke in the kitchen. It was a routine for them. For the remaining time, they might smoke together or smoke individually based on personal needs. Smoking inside the kitchen was a rather normal activity for chefs.

Firm U's karaoke was on the upper floor; I later found that smoking on the upper floor was more significant. Karaoke customers could freely smoke inside karaoke rooms and in the lobby. Nobody had ever prevented them from smoking. Firm U even provided ashtrays for them. In the second week, I one day asked Wen, the head chef, why they were allowed to smoke in the kitchen. Wen said:

> It's okay. See, there is a gap between the two pieces of doors. The air can pass in from outside. He (the owner) already removed the smoke detectors for both floors. The circuit inside the sensor has been cut off. That's for us to smoke. It's a Chinese restaurant. The law is only set to regulate British restaurants. That's fine.

According to Wen's description, which I had to take at face-value, it was the owner who cut off the circuit to pave the way for chefs and karaoke customers to smoke. Similar to the perceptions from Zha, Juan and Yi, Wen also separated 'Chinese restaurants' from 'British restaurants'. They all believed that Chinese restaurants were immune to British regulations and laws. They had their ways of dealing with varieties of issues, regardless of types of legislation.

As frequently mentioned in previous chapters, Firm U's owner appeared every one or two weeks because he had two other restaurants in Manchester. One day during the 'smoking time' after lunch, the owner suddenly arrived. Because everybody was smoking in the corner, nobody knew the owner had gone into the kitchen. When the owner appeared, the chefs said hello to the owner. The owner instructed:

Go to bring in the oil and lamb from my car.

Having said this, the owner walked away. After hearing the owner's words, everybody put out their cigarettes and went out. This was an extremely smooth process. There was no comment from the owner on smoking at all. It was obvious that the owner treated smoking inside the kitchen as a legitimate behaviour.

During Firm U's re-decoration period, it was only Yi and I who regularly worked in the kitchen. One day when we were cleaning, a man went into the kitchen and started to chat with Yi in Cantonese. It was obvious that they knew each other. After about ten minutes, the man lit a cigarette and passed one to Yi. They began to smoke in the centre of the kitchen. The man stayed that afternoon for about an hour. They smoked three times, either beside the hob or beside the operation table.

After my intensive fieldwork in Firm U, I regularly went back to get updates. One day when I walked into Firm U's kitchen, Yi was there. I asked him whether there was any latest news, Yi said to me:

> Several days ago, officers from the health department went to check Firm A's hygiene condition (both Firm U and Firm A were located in the 'China Town' area). Before they left, they found a cigarette butt in the kitchen. Firm A was forced to shut immediately.

Having said this, Yi lit a cigarette. After he had finished smoking, Yi carefully cleaned the floor and threw the butt into the bin. Previously, there was an ashtray on the floor, and the ash was everywhere on the floor. However, I noticed that the ashtray was missing, and Yi's cleaning of the floor also surprised me.

Firm A's closure demonstrated that smoking inside the kitchen did not just occur in Firm U. Chefs in Firm A definitely also smoked in the kitchen. Otherwise, there would not have been a butt identified by officers from the floor. The regulation for sure had its effects once the violation had been caught. However, this did not stop Yi from smoking inside the kitchen. The violation of the Health Act continued in Firm U.

The Employment of Alleged Illegal Workers

When discussing the conflict between Mandarin speaking workers and Cantonese speaking workers in Chapter 5, it mentioned that Cantonese speaking chefs holding a UK passport would like to cause Teng's employment to be terminated by informing the city council that he was an illegal worker. According to Teng's words, his visa was originally signed to a Chinese restaurant in Cambridge. Due to his departure from Cambridge without permission from the immigration office, he believed that his visa must have been cancelled.

During Firm U's refurbishment period, I one day had a meal with Teng to get updates on Firm U. Teng told me:

> I'm now considering giving up the current job and moving to Nottingham. The immigration office has been recently investigating illegal workers in Chinese restaurants (in Sheffield). Once I was caught, I would be expelled immediately. There is no immigration office in Nottingham. So, I'm considering moving to Nottingham. Last week, I heard that the head chef in Firm T had left for a break in case of being caught. To be honest, I'm now so worried. That's why I transferred all my earnings to China last week. Once I was caught, if I hadn't transferred that money, I would have lost everything. Anyway, the current situation is really intense. My friend in Nottingham is now searching for a job for me. Once he finds me a decent job, I will leave for Nottingham.

A week after Firm U re-opened, when Teng had left Firm U, Yi one day asked me whether I had any news about Teng. I told him that two days ago, Teng's WeChat (Chinese version of WhatsApp) showed that he was in Winchester. Yi said in a teasing tone:

> So, this means he has changed his workplace again. I heard that he was in Liverpool in the beginning, then Leeds. You said that he had told you he was in Newcastle. Now, he is in Winchester. You know what? The biggest problem for him is that he is an illegal worker. Not many owners would take the risk to use him.
>
> The policy changed several years ago. Previously, once you were caught, you just said you forgot to take your ID card. Or, for example, I have a UK passport. You can use my information. That was fine. In 2011, it changed fundamentally. The government began to use fingerprints. There is no chance for any illegal worker to survive once they are caught. His visa was signed to London, right? You know what? Since 2011, the wage for newly arrived labour has been paid by bank card so that they have to pay the tax. I once asked him whether he had a bank card. He said no. I asked him whether he had ever paid tax. He answered no, as well. It's no doubt his visa has been cancelled. He has been on the blacklist of the immigration office. It's just about time. See when he will be caught.

About two weeks later, Teng one day sent me a message telling me that he might come to Sheffield on his day off. I asked him where he was working. He texted:

> I'm now in a small town.
>> It's far from the city centre, so nobody would come here to investigate. It's safe here.
>> No restaurants within the city would take the risk to employ me, and meanwhile I don't want to leave myself in the risk of being caught as well.

With the progress of technology, an illegal worker was unlikely to escape the inspection. Once they were caught, there would be a one-way ticket to China. The status of illegal workers was regarded by Yi as a huge risk. In the face of a potential investigation, Teng frequently changed his work-places to avoid inspection. Both Yi and Teng's words also indicated that a potential breach of the law resulting from the employment of individuals who were alleged to be illegal workers might also cause trouble for owners.

Chapter 3 mentioned that Yi had been dissatisfied with the owner as the owner's decision conflicted with Yi's preferences about how to organise the buffet:

> If he continues to make me feel unhappy, I will have the restaurant closed, plus his two restaurants in Manchester. Last time, Chong (a driver) told me that he had altogether eight illegal workers in his two restaurants in Manchester. One illegal worker would cause him to pay £20K. Then, let him prepare the money.
>
> I once told you that if I would like him (the owner) to sack Teng, he must go. Do you understand? If we are unhappy, we then report this to the council. £20K for one. It would be altogether £40K for him and his wife. Can he (the owner) not sack him (Teng)? Anyway, there is no need to do this if things do not go that far.

With the risk of being fined, owners might make cautious decisions about whether to employ illegal workers. If the potential price for employing illegal labour was massive, why were some Chinese restaurants owners reported to still employ illegal workers? Bearing this question in mind, I one day talked with Zha, Firm U's front area manager. He said:

> Erm, there are fewer illegal workers than before. Previously, it was the convention to use illegal workers because illegal workers were cheaper. However, the margin has reduced a lot nowadays. Moreover,

supervision on illegal workers was not very intense previously. If officers catch you, you can just say you have a few days off from your workplace and work here as a part-time worker. Or, you can just sit in the front area as if you are a customer. They do not investigate customers. However, after the change of the policy (the introduction of fingerprints identification), the cheating no longer works. I do not know why he (the owner) still uses illegal workers. See, there is no big difference in wages. Anyway, fewer and fewer Chinese restaurants would choose to use illegal workers.

The actual wage level was indeed no different from Teng to other kitchen assistants. They all earned £300 a week. Chapter 4 discussed the background of the recruitment of Teng. Due to the sudden departure of Firm U's two kitchen workers and the shortage of labour supply in Sheffield, the owner got Teng from the internet. By discussing the NMW breach, the WTR breach and the Health Act breach, it suggested that the owners did not take regulation as a serious matter. The employment of Teng, as an alleged illegal worker, further demonstrated that when facing difficulties arising from the external environments, the regulation was something that could be ignored.

On the whole, the pressure upon employing illegal workers had greater constraints over both employers and employees' choices compared to other potential breaches. An illegal worker could be easily identified with solid proof. Both workers and owners would suffer hugely after being caught. Thus, owners and workers in the ethnic Chinese restaurant sector took this violation seriously. However, even in a situation like this, there were still owners who were willing to run the risk of employing allegedly illegal workers.

Conclusions

This chapter discussed how informality interacted with ethnicity in the ethnic Chinese restaurant sector. Informality has frequently been regarded as the nature of small firm employment relations, with limited use of written policies and practices, and an ad hoc way of management (Ram et al., 2001; Marlow, 2003). As one of the defining characteristics in small firms, informality was also present in the two case study firms. It was reflected throughout the human resource management practices. The order was negotiated between owners and workers in a continuous process on the shop floor, influenced by a range of external factors and internal forces.

The informal mechanism in small firms created space for workers to reinterpret control through the process of negotiation (Moule, 1998). This chapter summarised three types of fiddles practised in the two restaurants. It demonstrated that the informal management system left much room for workers to modify the rules. For some fiddles, they were conducted by taking advantage of the informal management structure for their interests. For other fiddles, they were practised as resistance to management control. 'Cheating by informal connection' reflected how the informal network of recruitment enabled workers to cheat the system. The 'intergroup cheating' represented the collaboration, deliberate or not, between front area managers and kitchen workers, which reflected a lack of solidarity between owners and co-ethnic workers. Thus, cheating in the ethnic Chinese restaurant sector was complex. It was the interaction between informality and a series of external and internal factors.

This chapter also discussed how owners and workers in the ethnic Chinese restaurant sector responded to a variety of UK laws. This research examined four aspects of employment practices in relation to laws and regulations. They were: the national minimum wage, working time for student workers, health and safety issues, and alleged employment of illegal workers. It was suggested by participants' descriptions that the violation of laws and regulations existed in all of the four aspects. Although informal practices involving law breach did exist in South-Asian small firms, it was largely because they were forced to engage in illegal practices, and it was not very common among them (Ram et al., 2000; Jones et al., 2006). By contrast, quite a few workers in the ethnic Chinese restaurant sector regarded the breach of laws as 'legitimate'. They explicitly expressed that the law was only set up to regulate British restaurants instead of Chinese restaurants. The actual labour management practices, as described by them, were rarely developed to take regulations into consideration. During this process, co-operation between employers and employees played a central part in providing a solid foundation for violation. The strong co-operation between these two parties was, however, extremely rare in relation to other activities. These ethnic Chinese restaurants operated as if they were in China. From this sense, it was as if they were 'Chinese ambassadors' in the UK. Although they were in the UK setting, the UK law placed very few constraints upon them.

7   Discussion

Despite the rapid increase of ethnic businesses from diverse origins in Britain over the past decades, little intensive research has been conducted to focus on the workplace level to interpret management practices and employment relationships in ethnic Chinese small firms. In addressing the research gap, this study aims to examine the nature of employment relations in the ethnic Chinese restaurant sector in the UK context. It set out four empirical chapters—influences from the product market, influences from the labour market, multi-cultural workforces and the interaction between informality and ethnicity—to discuss how management and workplace relations were experienced in the context.

The concluding chapter begins by briefly reviewing the findings of the research. Section 2 synthesises these findings and discusses empirical insights. Section 3 will draw out the key concepts from the study and connect them to existing frameworks to explore theoretical generalisations. The final section is to discuss the methodological significances of the research for future studies.

Summarising the Findings

The Chinese restaurant sector in Sheffield has experienced a significant increase in both the demand side and supply side over the past ten years. For the demand side, there was a continuous rise of Chinese students from 2008 to 2013. For the supply side, a large number of chefs went to start their own businesses. The demand fluctuated heavily over a year's time. This was due to the frequent change of Chinese student numbers following the patterns of semester time, as students accounted for the majority of customers. This demand fluctuation influenced owner-managers' management practices to a large extent. Staff recruitment and dismissal completely followed the demand change. However, actual adaptation could not always fit into the demand fluctuation model. In order to control the labour costs, the practical labour management practices always led to two types of problems: early adjustment (employee dismissal before the transition from a high demand period to a low demand period) and late adjustment (employee recruitment after the transition from a low demand period to a high demand period). The consequence was that there had been fewer workers than the two restaurants actually needed, which caused massive problems in management and created dramatic tensions between owners and workers.

With the continuing increase of new Chinese restaurants, saturation became the major problem. In five years from 2011 to 2015, the number of Chinese restaurants in the university area rose from three to over 15. The sector, as a result, experienced intense competition. The competitive market largely constrained owners' choices in pricing strategies and the ways of serving customers. Moving upward might be a strategic choice for owner-managers as most competed in the down-market. However, it required a large amount of capital, which was hard to achieve for chefs as the co-owners.

With a large number of chefs establishing their restaurants, there had been a seriously short supply of kitchen workers in the ethnic Chinese restaurant sector in Sheffield. The study examined management practices and power dynamics between owners and different groups of workers under the particular labour market situation.

Ethnic Chinese restaurant owners had high levels of dependence upon chefs. With the supply shortage from the labour market, recruiting a skilled chef was not an easy task. Firm U failed to introduce the buffet as the owner could not find proper chefs for three months. Firm D's owner even tolerated workers' cheating and fiddles as she was unwilling to have a direct conflict with chefs in fear of their departure. Chefs' dominant labour market position provided them with strong negotiation power over wage-effort bargaining. They actively engaged with direct negotiation for their interests. Owners' authority was challenged on a variety of occasions.

By contrast, kitchen assistants were in a weak labour market position with owners' low level of dependence on them although the ethnic Chinese restaurant sector also faced a labour shortage for kitchen assistants. Owner-managers imposed harsh control upon them. Kitchen assistants' subordinate position largely constrained their bargaining power. Negotiation over wage was not acceptable by owners. None of the kitchen assistants successfully negotiated for a pay rise during the period of my fieldwork. When experiencing the product market fluctuation, their job security was also affected significantly. Workers had little choice but to be compliant with owners' decisions.

In the specific context of the ethnic Chinese restaurant sector, it mainly consisted of three groups: Mandarin speakers, Cantonese speakers and

British-born Chinese. The study examined how multi-cultural workforces influenced employment relationships and labour management practices. The first problem arising from multi-cultural workforces was communication difficulty. As different languages were being spoken, direct verbal communication was sometimes difficult between members of different groups. In Firm D, because of the language barrier, guessing became a regular practice for employees trying to understand the owner's words. Intersubjectivity significantly influenced employees' behaviours in responding to the owner's words. However, the accommodation based on guessing in practice could not always catch up with the owner's real meanings. Once mistakes occurred due to misunderstanding, what followed next would be conflicts and tensions between the owner and employees.

Under the multi-cultural working environment, owners' trust towards workers from different groups was considerably different. Employees from other groups were believed untrustworthy for both owners. Although Firm U's owner could understand and speak Cantonese, he had low trust in Cantonese speakers. The owner of Firm D was from Hong Kong with a Cantonese background. In practice, only the Cantonese speaking part-time front area worker had access to the till. The assumptions and prejudices largely shaped their attitudes and labour management practices towards workers from different backgrounds.

The key focus was to examine the extent of conflicts between members from different cultural groups and the significance of their shop floor behaviours. The empirical data revealed that explicit conflicts existed between Mandarin speaking workers and Cantonese speaking workers. Workers from the two groups engaged in frequent argument and struggle. With the cultural and language differences, members of one group had substantial hatred towards the other group. Their shop floor behaviours were seriously shaped by this type of hostility and antagonism. An awareness of the tensions between groups from different regions was crucial to explain co-operation and conflicts at the point of production.

The last focus of the study was the integration between informality and ethnicity. Informal practices dominated management processes in both Firm D and Firm U. In exploring the dynamics of informality, examples illustrated how work was structured in ad hoc ways with the bargained nature. The order was negotiated continuously with the influence from both external and internal variables. Informality in the ethnic Chinese restaurant sector interacted with ethno-cultural forces such as the limited level of contribution and loyalty from co-ethnic workers in shaping different types of workplace fiddles.

The analysis also discussed how owners and workers responded to a variety of UK laws. It examined four aspects of employment practices in relation to laws and regulations—the NMW, the WTR, health and safety, and alleged employment of illegal workers. Law breaches, according to the participants' accounts, existed in all of these four aspects. Quite a few employees regarded the breach of laws as 'legitimate'. Their ethnic Chinese background made them share the common idea that the laws were only set to regulate British restaurants, instead of Chinese restaurants. Co-operation between employers and employees provided a solid foundation for violations, which formed different patterns of workplace relations between the two parties. The concept of the 'Chinese ambassadors' was developed to describe these ethnic Chinese restaurants. Although these restaurants were in the UK setting, the UK laws placed few constraints upon them in practice. From this sense, it was as if they were 'Chinese ambassadors' in the UK.

Empirical Insights

The Nature of the Ethnic Chinese Restaurant Sector

Having acknowledged the complexity and heterogeneity of employment relations in small firms, the research chose one up-market restaurant and one down-market restaurant as the research sites, aiming to capture variation under different situations and explore subsequent significances to management practices and workplace relations. It was expected that there might be different patterns of control strategies and social relations (Edwards, 1995; Jones et al., 2006). However, as shown from the empirical data, management in Firm D and Firm U was generally conducted in the same ways, and shop floor dynamics between owner-managers and workers in the two restaurants also shared common characteristics to a large extent.

First, the nature of the product market in the sector was highly competitive and fluctuated. Under the same environment of intense competition and frequent demand fluctuation, owner-managers' choices were influenced mostly in the same way. The competitive environment meant that their pricing strategy had to match the same level as their competitors', and their primary concern was to reduce labour costs as much as possible. Their recruitment, dismissal and training practices were the same to adapt to the demand change. Second, the whole sector experienced a labour shortage for kitchen workers. Front area workers were all part-time students. Workers' negotiating power in both of the restaurants was largely dependent on their labour market positions.

Thus, the two restaurants operated within a similar external environment, and they had exactly the same type of employee profile. It seemed that the distinction between one that was a little lower and the other that was a little higher was overridden. It was less to do with the subtle distinction within this particular context. The deciding features were whether the restaurant was in busy periods or non-busy periods and whether a worker was a chef or a kitchen assistant. These were the fundamental factors to shape employment relations in the two firms. It was not necessarily about whether it was a higher-end restaurant or a lower-end restaurant. The distinction between up-market and down-market was almost a misleading clue in the beginning. In practice, that level of subtlety did not exist. Management strategies were largely decided by the unstable and intensively competitive product market. Employees' effort bargaining and negotiated power were dependent upon their labour market positions. The two restaurants had dramatic similarities in how they were run. They were fairly similar, regardless of the difference in their market positions. The markets exerted significant pressures over management and employment relations. It indicated how the nature of the ethnic Chinese restaurant sector influenced managerial practices and shop floor experiences. It was the industry that significantly shaped the employment relations and workplace behaviours, not their particular market positions.

Ethnic Twist—the Nature of Shared Ethnicity

Apart from a pot washer in Firm U from Portugal, all of the workers in the two firms were ethnic Chinese. Being an ethnic Chinese person almost appeared to be the prerequisite for working in a Chinese restaurant. Ethnicity had the highest priority for getting an entry in the sector. Another issue that was strongly linked to shared ethnicity was the regulation breach. The alleged widespread violation of laws was attributed to their identity of being ethnic Chinese. Laws and regulations were believed by many participants to only constrain British businesses, instead of Chinese businesses. Shared ethnicity bonded owners and workers together to breach the law collaboratively. However, except for these two aspects, shared ethnicity within the ethnic Chinese context seemed to influence workplace relationships negatively.

Chan et al. (2007) indicated that co-ethnicity within the ethnic Chinese community should not be interpreted simply to mean it is a homogeneous group. However, there was no detailed explanation of the dynamics between different group numbers. This research went further than just identifying the problem. Empirical data from the fieldwork have illustrated that an inherent antagonism between Mandarin speaking workers and Cantonese speaking workers strongly shaped their behaviours. Conflicts and struggle were frequent on the shop floor between different group members. With different traditions, different language being spoken and different perceptions of people from different parts of the country, their workplace relationships were negatively impacted by shared ethnicity. Existing literature focusing on South Asian small firms has demonstrated that ethnic minority firms were generally involved with kinship ties. Although workers within the same community might not be exactly family members, they shared the family culture and subsequent ethnic tie. The importance of kinship and ethnic ties in supporting the initiation and development of ethnic minority enterprises was confirmed (Ram et al., 2000; Jones et al., 2006). Although subsequent studies acknowledged that ethnic minority businesses were also largely shaped by the wider political-economic environment, the importance of how ethno-cultural features and shared ethnicity positively helped to bond owners and workers in ethnic small firms could not be denied (Kloosterman, 2010; Jones et al., 2014). Recognising the impact from the wider context was not intended to eliminate the role of social capital of ethnic ties (Jones et al., 2012). By contrast, within the ethnic Chinese group, while to outsiders China may appear a somewhat homogenous entity, historical tensions and traditional divisions persisted, alongside a particular regional sense of kinship. The regional tie was basically reflected as the conflict between Northern people speaking Mandarin and Southern people (particularly people from Guangdong province and Hong Kong) speaking Cantonese. Furthermore, struggle also existed between Mandarin speaking workers from different regions (provinces).

In the Chinese restaurant sector, co-ethnicity and ethnic ties were two distinct concepts. Co-ethnicity in this context did not give rise to ethnic ties. The social relations as far as the co-ethnicity was concerned was not just about the country of origin or the ethnic Chinese heritage. The point of co-ethnicity or shared ethnicity within this context was too broad. Regional identity was the over-riding factor influencing how workers perceived others, reflecting whether a person was from the north or the south, what language was being spoken and what cultural characteristics were being shared. Co-ethnicity and so-called ethnic ties had little impacts on behaviours in the workplace. Regional ties were much more significant once workers were inside the firms. In the Chinese workforce, 'region' had profound implications to affect shop floor relations between employers and employees.

Based on the analysis, the concept of 'ethnic twist' was drawn out. The ethnic twist, in this context, referred to the conflict and antagonism between Cantonese speaking employees from the Southern area and Mandarin speaking employees from the Northern area. It was the region and language that had major impacts. The regional gap, the language difference and the cultural diversity altogether developed barriers between employees from different groups. In the day-to-day operation of the firms, the importance of shared ethnicity gave way to other factors. Co-ethnicity was trumped by the markets and regional ties in the ethnic Chinese restaurant sector. Everybody was ethnic Chinese, but it had evolved to affect working experiences. Co-ethnicity in this instance seemed to be a double-edged sword. It helped ethnic Chinese to get into the workplace. However, once they were inside these businesses, shared ethnicity worked more as a constraining factor to connect people. It was the ethnic twist that began to come into play. The ethnic twist negatively influenced social relations between different group members during their day-to-day work.

Students: A Specific Resource for Ethnic Chinese Restaurant Owners

Women's labour has been regarded as the key resource in the success of ethnic businesses (Ram, 1994; Carter et al., 2015; Ram et al., 2017a). First, the cost of female workers was generally cheap because most of them were family and community labour with a dependent relationship with men. Second, due to their subordinate position, the survival of ethnic businesses was largely sustained upon the exploitation of minority women. Female labour was, therefore, a crucial source for South Asian small enterprises. While in the ethnic Chinese restaurant sector, it was the students who provided true value for owners.

In the two restaurants, 100% of part-time workers in the front area was students. Chinese students provided a pool of candidates who would like to get a part-time job. This primarily solved the problem of recruitment from the labour market. Owner-managers could find replacements easily from their waiting lists. As front area servicing work did not require specific ability, under a situation with sufficient supply of potential workers, Chinese restaurant owners had little dependence upon workers. Front area workers could be dropped from the roster at any time, for any reason, decided by either owners' or managers' perceptions. Work security of student workers was completely vulnerable. Student workers had little power in the face of imposed control. This environment, therefore, enabled owners with strong power in dictating the relations, which eased their management pressure considerably.

Moreover, by employing students, owners could save significant amounts of labour costs. In both of the two case study firms, front area student workers were all paid £5 per hour, compared to an average of £6 for full-time managers. The research has demonstrated that the priority for owners in management was to reduce labour costs. In a context where they had limited choice in pricing strategies, the labour cost was one of the few variables they could actively control. Furthermore, part-time student workers enabled owner-managers to exert flexible control. Owners could adjust the number of workers hourly according to customer demand change each day.

For example, although the evening shift was set from 6 PM to 10 PM in firm D, it was not common that employees would finish at 10 PM. The owner normally stopped their work at 8 PM or 9 PM as firm D had fewer customers on evening shifts. In responding to the product market fluctuation during a year's time, owners could adapt to the demand change swiftly by employing part-time workers. This type of easy replacement and dismissal could otherwise have been difficult to conduct if they had employed full-time workers. Consequently, with less pay for each member and flexible control, ethnic Chinese restaurant owners could reduce labour costs significantly by employing students as part-time service workers. Students were a true resource for Chinese restaurant owners.

Indeed, ethnic Chinese restaurants were also valuable for students. Nearly all of the student workers in the two restaurants stated that the fundamental reason for them to find a part-time job was to get extra money to balance economic pressures. However, their average English level was not adequate to earn them a job in most non-Chinese businesses. The ethnic constraint was largely solved under the economic environment with growing numbers of Chinese restaurants. Despite receiving a wage under the NMW, students appreciated that Chinese restaurants provided them with the opportunity to get a part-time job.

Theoretical Generalisation

Chapter 2 discussed two conceptual frameworks—Harney and Dundon's framework (Harney and Dundon, 2006), and Gilman and Edwards's framework (Gilman and Edwards's, 2008). They developed from the traditional debate about how employment relations in small firms are shaped by a variety of factors. These two frameworks are similar in that they both demonstrate that there is a range of competing factors, both externally and internally, that have impacts upon management practices and employment relationships in small firms. Under certain environments, some might be more influential, while the others might be less influential, which reflects the context-sensitive view in understanding how different contexts have meanings to employment relations in small firms (Ram and Edwards, 2010).

In the context of ethnic minority enterprises, it has been widely acknowledged that management strategies and employment relationships in ethnic businesses were the results of the interplay between ethnic resources and structural influences (Kloosterman, 2010; Edwards et al., 2016; Kemeny, 2017). Building on existing research, Figure 7.1 summarises the existing analytical framework used to guide empirical research in studying employment relations in ethnic minority enterprises.

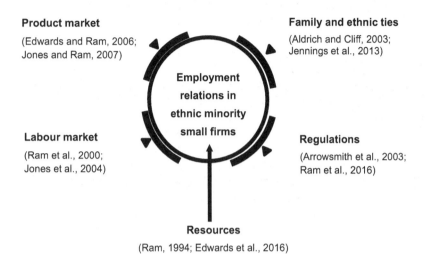

Figure 7.1 The Analytical Framework for Existing Research

The framework consists of five key aspects that are believed to have major impacts on management practices and employment relationships in ethnic minority small firms. The five themes are: the product market, the labour market, family and ethnic ties, regulations and resources. These factors do not exist independently; they relate to each other to some extent with potential influences. Tensions between these variables are negotiated on a day-to-day basis, shaping categories such as strategic choices and management styles.

This study reveals that the dimensions of the product market, the labour market and regulations had various degrees of influences on management–worker relations in the ethnic Chinese restaurant sector. Students as a particular resource significantly sustained the development of the sector.

There remains one theme arising from the research to be analysed: the multi-cultural workforces. The key concept drawn out from discussing the multi-cultural workforces is 'ethnic twist'. It reflects the conflict between workers from different groups, with the different language being spoken and different cultural background. What lies behind the 'ethnic twist' is the concept of 'regional ties', which replaces 'family ties' or 'ethnic ties' in shaping workers' behaviours and attitudes in the ethnic Chinese restaurant sector. By exploring the heterogeneity of people in the ethnic Chinese restaurant sector and drawing out the concept of 'ethnic twist', it can throw light on future research to discover how struggle and antagonism within ethnic groups shapes patterns of workplace behaviours.

Based on the discussion above, a new theoretical framework designed for future research in studying employment relations ethnic minority small business is developed and shown in Figure 7.2.

Compared to the framework used to structure existing research, this new framework remains 'the product market', 'the labour market', 'regulations' 'family and ethnic ties' and 'resource' themes. The 'ethnic twist' has been added to the new framework. The concept denotes that co-ethnic workers cannot simply be treated as a homogeneous group. The different backgrounds and cultures might have significant negative impacts on their attitudes and behaviours towards others. It is necessary to recognise the heterogeneity between group members and examine how the difference shapes shop floor behaviours. This revised framework is developed as a guide for researchers who study small firms with people from different ethnic groups. The addition of the concept of 'ethnic twist' expands the current understanding of patterns of employment relations in ethnic minority small firms. The revised framework, therefore, identifies a new category that might have major effects in ethnic minority small firms.

Edwards et al. (2006) noted that a framework needs to be sensitive to the environment in which firms operate. Although a theoretical model can guide empirical research, this does not necessarily mean that all of the dimensions

Figure 7.2 The Analytical Framework Suggested for Future Research

will be highly influential in a given context (Wapshott and Mallett, 2016). For example, in the ethnic Chinese restaurant sector, it is the 'ethnic twist' instead of 'ethnic ties' that strongly shapes the management practices and shop floor dynamics. Subsequent research is expected to adapt this model in studying ethnic minority businesses. The key themes in the framework provide an analytical basis for exploring employment relations in small firms from different ethnic groups. What is more important is to capture the dimensions of these themes in various contexts. This requires researchers to examine how particular factors influence the shop floor behaviours and what factors might have more significant effects in one context while less in another context. The framework allows for comparison and contrast of how the context difference can shape their management practices and workplace relations. Thus, researchers should recognise subtle changes when applying this model for future research and it might be interesting to examine how 'ethnic twist' functions in different ways in other ethnic groups.

Methodological Implications

As a piece of study to examine workplace relations, this research is located within a rich ethnographic tradition (Roy, 1952, 1954; Lupton, 1963; Burawoy, 1979; Ram, 1994). By directly observing the process of production, ethnographic researchers have provided penetrating and novel insights into the dynamics of workplace relations. As noted by Ram and Edwards (2010), empirical studies and the ethnographic character of work have been illuminating subtle understandings of patterns of control in small firms. In Wapshott and Mallett's (2016) book, the authors suggested future directions for studies in small enterprises:

> In order to develop a more detailed understanding of practices in use, we would like to see more empirically rich ethnographic studies that seek to understand and explain the employment relationships and practices found in SMEs in different contexts.
>
> (Wapshott and Mallett, 2016, pp. 145)

With applying the ethnographic approach, I conducted an over seven-month participant observation in two Chinese restaurants as a fully functioning member. This enabled me to gain an in-depth understanding of the contexts and people's behaviours on a day-to-day basis. The study has revealed the heterogeneity of Chinese workers and the importance of culture and language as influences on relations between different groups of workers and between workers and managers. The insights provided by this research could not have been generated through alternative research approaches, such as surveys and interviews. The dynamics of conflicts between group members could arguably be only captured by being saturated into the fields and working closely with those participants. In-depth data collected from this study illustrated how the perception of regional ties strongly shaped managerial choices. For example, Firm U's owner sacked one worker in charge of karaoke by using him just one day completely due to lack of trust, as the worker was a Cantonese speaker while the owner himself was a Mandarin speaker. The ethnographic approach contributes to unravel the continuous tensions among people with various backgrounds on the shop floor and explain how behaviours were influenced by the tensions. Without an understanding of the nature of the dynamics, it would have been failing to draw out the concept of 'ethnic twist' to interpret the struggle inherent in the multi-cultural workforces and its implications, an area that has not been fully understood.

Similarly, the research examined the complex ways in which employers and employees were alleged to collaborate to breach regulations, management problems arising from the adjustment to the demand fluctuation, different types of fiddles conducted by employees, etc. These practices and their meanings hardly can be gained by using alternative methods. The ethnographic approach provides empirical support to uncover the complexities of labour management in the ethnic Chinese restaurant sector. Furthermore, the theoretical conception developed from the research is instrumental in guiding future research. This study, therefore, demonstrates the continued importance of the ethnographic approach in studying workplace relations.

Conclusions

This book contributes to existing knowledge by revealing the nature of employment relations in the ethnic Chinese restaurant sector in the UK context, a hitherto under-explored area. The study was organised and analysed in line with Ram and Edwards's (2010) 'two fronts' suggestion in advancing work on employment relations in small firms. Conceptually, this research embraced the core of industrial relations studies—conflict and consent. The analysis centred on how labour management practices regulate employees and how employees challenged these rules with the informal negotiation of order. Conflict and co-operation at the point of production were given continuous focus to examine the control process and explain patterns of accommodation in the two firms. Various sources of power, inside and outside the organisations, were discussed to shape the degrees of conflict and mutual adjustment between management and workers. With employers and employees using power to advance their interests, it analysed how the political process of management changed and developed under different situations. The analytical underpinning reflects the contested nature of employment relations in small firms.

Empirically, it grasped the social attributes to understand the nuances of management practices and employment relationships in the context. For instance, unlike patterns of employment influenced by gender and familial ties in South Asian small firms, it was the regional ties in the ethnic Chinese restaurant sector that played significant roles in affecting perceptions and beliefs. The assumption that people from different backgrounds were untrustworthy was taken for granted. This was central to form the struggle between Mandarin speaking workers and Cantonese speaking workers. These ethnic issues interacted with the economic-political environment to have impacts upon shop floor behaviours. The analysis in the whole demonstrates the importance of appreciating the interaction between external environments and internal forces in shaping outcomes in small businesses.

As for the future, it is expected to have more diverse research in studying employment relations in ethnic Chinese small businesses featuring different contexts. We see lots of literature discussing overseas Chinese firms in terms of cultural resources, business development, level of integration and structural constraints. Surprisingly little is published on interpretations of small firm workplace relations. This book might illuminate further studies to explore practices and employment relationships in ethnic Chinese small businesses in different national environments and industry sectors. Researchers could take a comparative approach by comparing and contrasting how differences arising from market positions, government policies and internal dynamics have various meanings to labour management and shop floor behaviours. By doing this, it is to achieve greater understandings of employment relations in ethnic Chinese small firms in modern economies and benefit a range of stakeholders such as investors and policymakers by gaining deeper knowledge in the field. Furthermore, it is interesting to see how the concept of 'ethnic twist' has implications for perceptions and behaviours in other ethnic minority enterprises and interacts with different themes to shape dynamics between owners and workers. Finally, given the importance of the rich ethnographic tradition in workplace studies, it suggests that future research should continue to engage with the possibilities of ethnographic studies to understand shop floor behaviours and workplace relations in small firms.

Bibliography

Aldrich, H. and Cliff, J. (2003). The Pervasive Effects of Family on Entrepreneurship: Toward a Family Embeddedness Perspective. *Journal of Business Venturing*. 18 (4), pp. 573–596.

Arrowsmith, J., Gilman, M. W., Edwards, P. and Ram, M. (2003). The Impact of the National Minimum Wage in Small Firms. *British Journal of Industrial Relations*. 41 (3), pp. 435–456.

ASE (Annual Survey of Entrepreneurs) (2016). *Sector, Gender, Ethnicity, Race, Veteran Status, and Employment Size of Firm*. Data: [https://factfinder.census.gov/faces/tableservices/jsf/pages/productview.xhtml?src=bkmk#]. Accessed: 15th June 2019.

Atkinson, C. (2008). An Exploration of Small Firm Psychological Contracts. *Work, Employment and Society*. 22 (3), pp. 447–465.

Barrett, G., Jones, T., McEvoy, D. and McGoldrick, C. (2002). The Economic Embeddedness of Immigrant Enterprise in Britain. *Industrial Journal of Entrepreneurial Behaviour and Research*. 18 (1), pp. 11–31.

Barrett, R. (1999). Industrial Relations in Small Firms: The Case of the Australian Information Industry. *Employee Relations*. 21 (3), pp. 311–324.

BIS (Department for Business, Innovation and Skills) (2014). *SME Business Barometer*. Data: [https://assets.publishing.service.gov.uk/government/uploads/system/uploads/attachment_data/file/298773/bis-14-p75a-sme-business-barometer-february-2014.pdf]. Accessed: 15th June 2019.

BIS (Department for Business, Innovation and Skills) (2018). *Business Population Estimates for the UK and Regions 2018*. Data: [https://assets.publishing.service.gov.uk/government/uploads/system/uploads/attachment_data/file/746599/OFFICIAL_SENSITIVE_-_BPE_2018_-_statistical_release_FINAL_FINAL.pdf]. Accessed: 15th June 2019.

Bolton Committee Report (1971). *Report of the Commission of Inquiry on Small Firms*. London: HMSO.

Bryman, A. and Bell, E. (2007). *Business Research Methods*. Oxford: Oxford University Press.

Burawoy, M. (1979). *Manufacturing Consent*. London: The University of Chicago Press.

Capelli, P. (1985). Theory Construction in Industrial Relations and Some Implications for Research. *Industrial Relations*. 24 (1), pp. 90–112.

Carter, S. (2011). The Rewards of Entrepreneurship: Exploring the Incomes, Wealth, and Economic Well-Being of Entrepreneurial Households. *Entrepreneurship Theory and Practice*. 35 (1), pp. 39–55.

Carter, S., Mason, C. and Tagg, S. (2009). Perceptions and Experience of Employment Regulation in UK Small Firms. *Environment and Planning C: Government and Policy*. 27 (2), pp. 267–278.

Carter, S., Mwaura, S., Ram, M., Thehan, K. and Jones, T. (2015). Barriers to Ethnic Minority and Women's Enterprise: Existing Evidence, Policy Tensions and Unsettled Questions. *International Small Business Journal*. 33 (1), pp. 49–69.

Chan, C. K., Cole, B. and Bowpitt, G. (2007). Beyond Silent Organisations: A Reflection of the UK Chinese People and Their Community Organisations. *Critical Social Policy*. 27 (4), pp. 509–533.

Chan, Y. M. and Chan, C. (1997). The Chinese in Britain. *Journal of Ethnic and Migration Studies*. 23 (1), pp. 123–131.

Chau, R. C. M. and Yu, S. W. K. (2001). Social Exclusion of Chinese People in Britain. *Critical Social Policy*. 21 (1), pp. 103–125.

Chaudhry, S. and Crick, D. (2004). The Business Practices of Small Chinese Restaurants in the UK: An Exploratory Investigation. *Strategic Change*. 13 (1), pp. 37–49.

Child, J. (1997). Strategic Choice in the Analysis of Action, Structure, Organizations and Environment: Retrospect and Prospect. *Organization Studies*. 18 (1), pp. 43–76.

Chiu, W. S. (1991). The Family Care of Chinese Old People, a Study of the Chinese Communities in London and Hong Kong. PhD Thesis, the University of Sheffield.

Clark, K. and Drinkwater, S. (2002). Enclaves, Neighbourhood Effects and Employment Outcomes: Ethnic Minorities in England and Wales. *Journal of Population Economics*. 15 (1), pp. 5–29.

Clark, K. and Drinkwater, S. (2010). Recent Trends in Minority Ethnic Entrepreneurship in Britain. *International Small Business Journal*. 28 (2), pp. 136–146.

Curran, J. and Stanworth, J. (1979). Worker Involvement and Social Relations in the Small Firm. *The Sociological Review*. 27 (2), pp. 317–342.

Dundon, T. and Wilkinson, A. (2009). HRM in Small and Medium-Sized Enterprises. In Collings, D. and Wood, G. (Eds.). *Human Resource Management: A Critical Approach*. London: Routledge.

Ecovis Beijing (2017). *Small and Medium Enterprises (SMEs) in China*. Data: [https://ecovis-beijing.com/smes-china/]. Accessed: 15th June 2019.

Edwards, P. (1995). From Industrial Relations to the Employment Relationship: The Development of Research in Britain. *Industrial Relations*. 50 (1), pp. 39–65.

Edwards, P. and Ram, M. (2006). Surviving on the Margins of the Economy: Working Relationships in Small, Low-Wage Firms. *Journal of Management Studies*. 43 (4), pp. 895–916.

Edwards, P. and Ram, M. (2010). HRM in Small Firms: Respecting and Regulating Informality. In Wilkinson, A., Bacon, N., Redman, T. and Snell, S. (Eds.). *The SAGE Hand Book of Human Resource Management*. London: SAGE Publications Ltd.

Edwards, P., Ram, M. and Black, J. (2004). Why Does Employment Regulation Not Damage Small Firms? *Journal of Law and Society.* 31 (2), pp. 245–265.

Edwards, P., Ram, M., Gupta, S. S. and Tsai, C. (2006). The Structure of Working Relationship in Small Firms: Towards a Formal Framework. *Organisation.* 13 (5), pp. 701–724.

Edwards, P., Ram, M., Jones, T. and Doldor, S. (2016). New Migrant Businesses and Their Workers: Developing, But Not Transforming, the Ethnic Economy. *Ethnic and Racial Studies.* 39 (9), pp. 1587–1617.

Edwards, P. K. and Scullion, H. (1982). *The Social Organisation of Industrial Conflict.* Oxford: Basil Blackwell Publisher.

Gerring, J. (2007). The Case Study: What It Is and What It Does. In Boix, C. and Stokes, S. C. (Eds.). *Oxford Handbook of Comparative Politics.* New York: Oxford University Press.

Gill, J. and Johnson, P. (2002). *Research Methods for Managers.* London: Sage Publications Ltd.

Gilman, M. W. and Edwards, P. K. (2008). Testing a Framework of the Organisation of Small Firms: Fast-Growth, High-Tech SMEs. *International Small Business Journal.* 26 (5), pp. 531–558.

Gilman, M. W, Edwards, P. K., Ram, M. and Arrowsmith, J. (2002). Pay Determination in Small Firms in the UK: The Case of the Response to the National Minimum Wage. *Industrial Relations Journal.* 33 (1), pp. 52–67.

Gold, R. (1958). Roles in Sociological Field Observations. *Social Forces.* 36 (3), pp. 217–223.

Goss, D. (1991a). *Small Business and Society.* London: Routledge.

Goss, D. (1991b). In Search of Small Firm Industrial Relations. In Burrows, R. (Eds.). *Deciphering the Enterprise Culture.* London: Routledge.

Gummesson, E. (2000). *Qualitative Methods in Management Research.* London: Sage Publications Ltd.

Hall, S., King, J. and Finlay, R. (2017). Migrant Infrastructure: Transaction Economies in Birmingham and Lecester, UK. *Urban Studies.* 54 (6), pp. 1311–1327.

Hammersley, M. (1998). *Reading Ethnographic Research.* Essex: Addison Wesley Longman Limited.

Hammersley, M. and Atkinson, P. (1995). *Ethnography: Principles in Practice.* London: Routledge.

Harney, B. and Dundon, T. (2006). Capturing Complexity: Developing an Integrated Approach to Analysing HRM in SMEs. *Human Resource Management Journal.* 16 (1), pp. 48–73.

Heath, A., Rothon, C. and Kilpi, E. (2008). The Second Generation in Western Europe: Education, Unemployment and Occupational Attainment. *Annual Review of Sociology.* 34 (1), pp. 211–235.

Health Act (2006). *Health Act 2006.* Data: [www.legislation.gov.uk/ukpga/2006/28/contents]. Accessed: 15th June 2019.

Heyes, J. and Gray, A. (2004). Small Firms and the National Minimum Wage: Implications for Pay and Training Practices in the British Private Service Sector. *Policy Studies.* 25 (3), pp. 209–225.

Holliday, R. (1995). *Investigating Small Firms: Nice Work?* London: Routledge.

House of Commons (1985). *Chinese Community in Britain: Second Report from the Home Affairs Committee Session 1985–1985*. London: HMSO.

Ingham, G. (1970). *Size of Organisation and Worker Behaviour*. Cambridge: Cambridge University Press.

Jennings, J., Breitkreuz, R. and James, A. (2013). When Family Members Are Also Business Owners: Is Entrepreneurship Good for Families? *Family Relations*. 62 (3), pp. 472–489.

Jones, T., Cater, J., Silva, D. and McEvoy, D. (1989). *Ethnic Business and Community Needs, Report to the Commission for Racial Equality*. Liverpool: Liverpool Polytechnic.

Jones, T. and Ram, M. (2007). Re-Embedding the Ethnic Agenda. *Work, Employment and Society*. 21 (3), pp. 439–457.

Jones, T. and Ram, M. (2010). Ethnic Variations on the Small Firm Labour Process. *International Small Business Journal*. 28 (2), pp. 163–173.

Jones, T., Ram, M. and Edwards, P. (2006). Shades of Grey in the Informal Economy. *International Journal of Sociology and Social Policy*. 26 (9–10), pp. 357–373.

Jones, T., Ram, M. and Edwards, P. (2012). New Migrant Enterprise: Novelty or Historical Continuity. *Urban Studies*. 49 (14), pp. 3159–3176.

Jones, T., Ram, M., Edwards, P., Kiselinchev, A. and Muchenje, L. (2014). Mixed Embeddedness and New Migrant Enterprise in the UK. *Entrepreneurship and Regional Development*. 26 (5–6), pp. 500–520.

Jones, T., Ram, M. and Theodorakopoulos, N. (2010). Transnationalism as a Force for Ethnic Minority Enterprise? The Case of Somalis in Leicester. *International Journal of Urban and Regional Research*. 34 (3), pp. 565–585.

Jones, T., Ram, M. and Villares-Varela, M. (2019). Diversity, Economic Development and New Migrant Entrepreneurs. *Urban Studies*. 56 (5), pp. 960–976.

Kemeny, T. (2017). Immigrant Diversity and Economic Performance in Cities. *International Regional Science*. 40 (2), pp. 164–208.

Kinnie, N., Purcell, J., Hutchinson, S., Terry, M., Collinson, M. and Scarbrough, H. (1999). Employment Relations in SMEs: Market-Driven or Customer Shaped? *Employee Relations*. 21 (3), pp. 218–235.

Kitching, J. (2006). A Burden on Business? Reviewing the Evidence Base on Regulation and Small-Business Performance. *Environment and Planning C: Government and Policy*. 24 (6), pp. 799–814.

Kloosterman, C. R. (2010). Matching Opportunities with Resources: A Framework for Analysing (Migrant) Entrepreneurship from a Mixed Embeddedness Perspective. *Entrepreneurship and Regional Development*. 22 (1), pp. 25–45.

Kloosterman, R., Van Der Leun, J. and Rath, J. (1999). Mixed Embeddedness: (In) formal Economic Activities and Immigrant Businesses in the Netherlands. *International Journal of Urban and Regional Research*. 23 (2), pp. 252–266.

Lee, R. (2019). Who Does the Dishes? Precarious Employment and Ethnic Solidarity among Restaurant Workers in Los Angeles' Chinese Enclave. *Ethnicities*. 19 (2), pp. 433–451.

Light, I. (2004). The Ethnic Ownership Economy. In Stiles, C. and Galbraith, C. (Eds.). *Ethnic Entrepreneurship: Structure and Process*. Oxford: Elsevier.

Luk, W. (2009). Chinese Ethnic Settlement in Britain: Spatial Meanings of an Orderly Distribution, 1981–2001. *Journal of Ethnic and Migration Studies*. 35 (4), pp. 575–599.

Lupton, T. (1963). *On the Shop Floor*. Oxford: Pergamon Press.

Marlow, S. (2002). Regulating Labour Management in Small Firms. *Human Resource Management Review*. 12 (3), pp. 25–43.

Marlow, S. (2003). Formality and Informality in Employment Relations: The Implications for Regulatory Compliance by Smaller Firms. *Environment and Planning C: Government and Policy*. 21 (4), pp. 531–547.

Marlow, S. (2005). Introduction. In Marlow, S., Patton, D. and Ram, M. (Eds.). *Managing Labour in Small Firms*. London: Routledge.

McMahon, J. (1996). Employee Relations in Small Firms in Ireland: An Exploratory Study of Small Manufacturing Firms. *Employee Relations*. 18 (5), pp. 66–80.

Mitchell, J. (1983). Case and Situation Analysis. *Sociological Review*. 31 (2), pp. 187–211.

Mok, T. M. and Platt, L. (2018). All Look the Same? Diversity of Labour Market Outcomes of Chinese Ethnic Group Populations in the UK. *Journal of Ethnic and Migration Studies*. 44 (1), pp. 1–21.

Moule, C. (1998). Regulation of Work in Small Firms: A View from the Inside. *Work, Employment and Society*. 12 (4), pp. 635–653.

Nadin, S. and Cassell, C. (2007). New Deal for Old? Exploring the Psychological Contract in a Small Firm Environment. *International Small Business Journal*. 25 (4), pp. 417–443.

National Minimum Wage (2015). *National Minimum Wage and National Living Wage rates*. Data: [www.gov.uk/national-minimum-wage-rates]. Accessed: 15th June 2019.

Ohri, S. and Faruqi, S. (1988). Racism, Employment and Unemployment. In Bhat, A., Carr-Hill, R. and Ohri, S. (Eds.). *Britain's Black Population: A New Perspective*. Aldershot: Gower.

ONS (Office for National Statistics) (2015). *2011 Census Analysis: Ethnicity and Religion of the Non-UK Born Population in England and Wales*. Data: [www.ons.gov.uk/peoplepopulationandcommunity/culturalidentity/ethnicity/articles/2011censusanalysisethnicityandreligionofthenonukbornpopulationinenglandandwales/2015-06-18]. Accessed: 15th June 2019.

OPCS (Office of Population Censuses and Surveys and General Register Office for Scotland) (1992). *Definitions: Great Britain*. London: HMSO.

Rainnie, A. (1989). *Small isn't Beautiful*. London: Routledge.

Ram, M. (1992). Coping with Racism: Asian Employers in the Inner-City. *Work, Employment and Society*. 6 (4), pp. 601–618.

Ram, M. (1994). *Managing to Survive*. Oxford: Blackwell.

Ram, M. (1996). Uncovering the Management Process: An Ethnographic Approach. *British Journal of Management*. 7 (1), pp. 35–44.

Ram, M. (1999). Managing Autonomy: Employment Relations in Small Professional Service Firms. *International Small Business Journal*. 17 (2), pp. 13–30.

Ram, M. and Edwards, P. (2003). Praising Caesar Not Burying Him: What We Know about Employment Relations in Small Firms. *Work, Employment and Society*. 17 (4), pp. 719–730.

Ram, M. and Edwards, P. (2010). Industrial Relations in Small Firms. In Colling, T. and Terry, M. (Eds.). *Industrial Relations: Theory and Practice*. Chichester: John Wiley and Sons, Ltd.

Ram, M., Edwards, P. and Jones, T. (2007). Staying Underground. Informal Work, Small Firms, and Employment Regulation in the United Kingdom. *Work and Occupations*. 34 (3), pp. 318–344.

Ram, M., Edwards, P., Gilman, M. and Arrowsmith, J. (2001). The Dynamics of Informality: Employment Relations in Small Firms and the Effects of Regulatory Change. *Work, Employment and Society*. 15 (4), pp. 845–861.

Ram, M., Edwards, P., Jones, T. and Villares-Varela, M. (2017b). From the Informal Economy to the Meaning of Informality: Developing Theory on Firms and Their Workers. *International Journal of Sociology and Social Policy*. 37 (7/8), pp. 361–373.

Ram, M. and Hillin, G. (1994). Achieving Break-Out: Developing Minority Businesses. *Journal of Small Businesses and Enterprise Development*. 1 (2), pp. 15–21.

Ram, M. and Holliday, R. (1993). Relative Merits: Family Culture and Kinship in Small Firms. *Sociology*. 27 (4), pp. 629–648.

Ram, M. and Jones, T. (2008). Ethnic Minority Business in the UK: A Review of Research and Policy Developments. *Environment and Planning C: Government and Policy Online*. 2 (3), pp. 163–171.

Ram, M., Jones, T., Abbas, T. and Sanghera, B. (2002). Ethnic Minority Enterprises in Its Urban Context: South Asian Restaurants in Birmingham. *International Journal of Urban and Regional Research*. 26 (1), pp. 24–40.

Ram, M., Jones, T. and Villares-Varela, M. (2017a). Migrant Entrepreneurship: Reflections on Research and Practice. *International Small Business Journal*. 35 (1), pp. 3–18.

Ram, M., Sanghera, B., Abbas, T., Barlow, G. and Jones, T. (2000). Ethnic Minority Business in Comparative Perspective: The Case of the Independent Restaurant Sector. *Journal of Ethnic and Migration Studies*. 26 (3), pp. 495–510.

Ram, M., Theodorakopoulos, N. and Jones, T. (2008). Forms of Capital, Mixed Embeddedness and Somali Enterprise. *Work, Employment and Society*. 22 (3), pp. 427–446.

Rochelle, T. and Marks, D. (2011). Health Behaviors and Use of Traditional Chinese Medicine Among the British Chinese. *Journal of Cross-Cultural Psychology*. 42 (3), pp. 390–405.

Rochelle, T. and Shardlow, S. (2013). Quality of Social Networks among UK Chinese. *Social Indicators Research*. 114 (2), pp. 425–439.

Rochelle, T. and Steven, S. (2013). Quality of Social Networks among UK Chinese. *Social Indicators Research*. 114 (2), pp. 425–439.

Roy, D. (1952). Quota Restriction and Goldbricking in a Machine Shop. *American Journal of Sociology*. 57 (5), pp. 427–442.

Roy, D. (1954). Efficiency and 'The Fix': Informal Intergroup Relations in a Piecework Machine Shop. *American Journal of Sociology*. 60 (3), pp. 255–266.

Runnymede Trust (1986). *The Chinese Community in Britain: The Home Affairs Committee Report in Context*. London: Runnymede Trust.

Scase, R. (2005). Managerial Strategies in Small Firms. In Marlow, S. (Ed.). *Managing Labour in Small Firms*. London: Routledge.

Scott, A. (1994). *Willing Slaves?* Cambridge: Cambridge University Press.

Scott, M. and Rainnie, A. (1982). Beyond Bolton: Industrial Relations in the Small Firm. In Stanworth, J., Westrip, A., Watkin, D. and Lewis, J. (Eds.). *Perspectives on a Decade of Small Business Research: Bolton 10 Years On*. Aldershot: Gower.

Secretary of State for the Home Department (1985). *The Government Reply to the Second Report from the Home Affairs Committee*. Session 1984–5. London: HMSO.

Sepulveda, L., Syrett, S. and Lyon, F. (2011). Population Superdiversity and New Migrant Enterprise: The Case of London. *Entrepreneurship and Regional Development*. 23 (7–8), pp. 469–497.

Sisson, K. (1993). In Search of Human Resource Management. *British Journal of Industrial Relations*. 31 (2), pp. 201–210.

Steinmetz, G. (2004). Odious Comparisons: Incommensurability, the Case Study, and 'Small N's' in Sociology. *Sociological Theory*. 22 (3), pp. 371–400.

Taylor, M. (1987). *Chinese Pupils in Britain: A Review of Research into the Education of Pupils of Chinese Origin*. Windsor: NFER-Nelson.

Tong, K. K., Hung, E. P. W. and Yuen, S. M. (2011). The Quality of Social Networks: Its Determinants and Impacts on Helping and Volunteering in Macao. *Social Indicators Research*. 102 (2), pp. 351–361.

Tsai, C. J., Sengupta, S. and Edwards, P. (2007). When and Why Is Small Beautiful? The Experience of Work in the Small Firm. *Human Relations*. 60 (12), pp. 1779–1807.

Tsang, E. (2014). Generalising from Research Findings: The Merits of Case Studies. *International Journal of Management Reviews*. 16 (4), pp. 369–383.

UKCISA (UK Council for International Student Affairs) (2019). International Student Statistics: UK Higher Education. Data: [www.ukcisa.org.uk/Research-Policy/Statistics/International-student-statistics-UK-higher-education]. Accessed: 15th June 2019.

UoS (University of Sheffield) (2019). *Institutional and Department student profiles*. Data: [https://apex-live.shef.ac.uk/pls/apex/f?p=136:1:::NO:::]. Accessed: 15th June 2019.

Vertovec, S. (2007). Super-Diversity and Its Implications. *Ethnic and Racial Studies*. 30 (6), pp. 1024–1054.

Wapshott, R. and Mallett, O. (2013). The Unspoken Side of Mutual Adjustment: Understanding Intersubjective Negotiation in Small Professional Service Firms. *International Small Business Journal*. 31 (8), pp. 978–996.

Wapshott, R. and Mallett, O. (2016). *Managing Human Resources in Small and Medium-Sized Enterprises*. Oxon: Routledge.

Ward, R. (1987). *Resistance, Accommodation and Advantage: Strategic Development in Ethnic Business*. Milton Keynes: Open University Press.

Ward, R. (1991). *Economic Development and Ethnic Business*. London: Routledge.

Watson, J. (1977). The Chinese: Hong Kong Villagers in the British Catering Trade. In Watson, J. (Eds.). *Between Two Cultures*. Oxford: Blackwell.

Werbner, P. (1984). *Business on Trust*. London: Cambridge University Press.

Werbner, P. (1994). Renewing an Industrial Past: British Pakistani Entrepreneurship in Manchester. In Brown, J. and Foot, R. (Eds.). *Migration: The Asian Experience*. New York: New York St. Martin's Press.

Wilkinson, A. (1999). Employment Relations in SMEs. *Employee Relations*. 21 (3), pp. 206–217.

Working Time Regulations (2003). *The Working Time Regulations*. Data: [www.hse. gov.uk/contact/faqs/workingtimedirective.htm]. Accessed: 15th June 2019.

Yin, R. K. (2009). *Case Study Research: Design and Methods*. California: Sage.

Index

Printed in the United States
by Baker & Taylor Publisher Services